Riding Rainbows

through the

Storms

Finding Perspective and Hope by Journaling Through a Pandemic

Pandemic problems concept, origami ship with surgical masks, #373957455 By Csaba Peterdi

By Anne Spry

Riding Rainbows through the Storms:
Finding Perspective and Hope by Journaling Through a Pandemic
By Anne Spry

Copyright © 2025 by Anne Spry
Paperback ISBN: 979-8-9889980-9-9
Ebook ISBN: 979-8-9927670-0-1
Library of Congress Control Number: 2024914902

Front cover image from Adobe Stock, _205570556, Lighthouse and Tornado. Photos and blog images in this book were produced by the author or purchased through Adobe Stock where noted.

Scripture passages are from the Revised Standard Version of the Bible, Copyright © 1946, 1952, and 1971, the Division of Christian Education of the National Council of the Churches of Christ in the United States of America. Used by permission. All rights reserved.

Some scripture passages are taken from the New American Standard Version of the Holy Bible, Copyright © 1960, 1971, 1977, 1995, 2020 by The Lockman Foundation. Used by permission. All rights reserved.

Personal Chapters Publishing - Wakarusa, KS
personalchapterspublishing.com

Praise for Riding Rainbows Through the Storms

Read this book and you'll experience the benefits of a new friendship. Author Anne Spry pours her heart and soul into this intriguing collection of personal journal entries, Kansas landscape photos, blogs, essays, and even a secret family recipe! A good friendship is full of love, support, humor, sorrow, pain, healing, gentle advice, and a willingness to share your authentic self–warts and all. *Riding Rainbows through the Storms* hits the mark on all these qualities.–**Thea Rademacher,** president, Flint Hills Publishing, and co-author of *A Drop in the Night, the Secret Mission of a WWII Airman*

To read Anne Spry's diary of pandemic pain and personal doubt is to recognize the walk that confronts every human, an individual journey of testing, of faith, and ultimately of growth. Filled with humility and leavened with humor and beautiful photographs, even a recipe, this journaling-as-coping-mechanism book reflects the many facets of ourselves. A deeply revealing and tender personal story.–**Ruth Maus,** author of *Lunacy and Acts of God, Valentine,* and *Puzzled.*

It is a rare experience to find one's own story captured on pages authored by another, but Anne Spry has done this beautifully in *Riding Rainbows.* This book is bound to be not only an award-winning memoir, but also a treasure trove for historians looking for clear, engaging, and descriptive documentation of what the Covid-19 pandemic was like for those of us who lived through it. Spry has managed to tell her own experiences in a way that allows those of us who didn't journal through the pandemic to feel as though we have. Every page, every musing, every observation she makes is common to us all. May God bless her for having the foresight, courage, and tenacity to capture on paper what the rest of us barely managed to endure.–**Cheri Battrick,** author of *Garage Sale of the Century* and *Journaling With Jesus: Writing to Heal from Trauma.*

It was like a poutpourri of emotions I felt as I read each page. This book moved me so much.–*B. J. Gray,* retired music educator

Even though I read this book during an especially busy time in my life, it was difficult to put it down once I started. Each entry brings up memories, emotions or thoughts that take me back to those days when we couldn't interact with others except on a computer screen or telephone. For many of us the pandemic was a mixed blessing. We lost so many things, even if temporarily. Like a lot of people, Anne talks of gaining something too–a closer relationship with God. Throughout her journal entries she talks about gaining a new appreciation for scripture and prayer. Peeking through it all you see how a relationship with God helps you get through the storms of life.–*Debbie Liddell,* pastor, Wakarusa Presbyterian Church

Contents

Hints of a Storm

"Keep your face always toward the sunshine, and shadows will fall behind you." — *Walt Whitman*

Prologue

I only see it now, in a retrospective reading of my journal entries from 2019–hints of the coming storm. I also see I was being prepared spiritually and mentally to face into a tsunami that would rock the world.

The tsunami referenced in this book, one that still seems to be affecting all our lives, is the pandemic. I dealt with Covid-19 infections, shutdowns, disruptions, social isolation and distancing, and even deaths of loved ones by pouring out my heart through my pen and my computer. Thank God for the healing tool of writing! It's something I've relied on my entire life.

I began journaling as a teen, writing out my troubles in a little black (to fit my bleak moods) book. I also kept a journal of my activities and troubles while serving as a Peace Corps volunteer in Brazil in the early 1970s. And despite being a newspaper editor and publisher for 27 years and having all kinds of writing out there for public consumption, I still kept a journal for my own private "therapy."

Journaling took me through the roller-coaster ride of emotions during a divorce from my first husband and my efforts to adjust to being a single mother. Recording my thoughts and feelings also took me through remarriage, moves, retirement from a satisfying career and a subsequent identity crisis. Who would I be now that I was no longer a newspaper editor and publisher? I remade myself through more writing, more journaling.

I began publishing blogs soon after retirement. I had written a personal column in the weekly newspaper I published for 27 years, so a blog was almost as natural to me as weekly deadlines. The blogging led to my first book, which was a collection of some of those personal columns. When I saw how satisfying it was to use my background to publish that first book, I began helping clients publish print-on-demand books.

Journaling, writing and helping clients was probably my salvation when facing into the storm of the sudden death of my second husband. Four years later, I remarried and moved. Those abrupt and major life milestones were all shared with my journals.

At that point in my life, I thought I had wrestled with and conquered a need to control the events and circumstances of my life. I thought I had found my purpose, my calling, and my true joy through my second husband, a move back to my ancestral home in Kansas, and making new writing friends. I had even discovered a new hobby of singing by joining a Sweet Adelines group.

Enter the pandemic in March of 2019. Everything in my life and the lives of everyone around me ground to a halt. Plans, social gatherings, babysitting my grandkids, meeting friends for lunch, going to church – it all stopped.

But thank God for the pandemic. It taught me so much, showed me so much. And it made me realize I had the best background any person can have in the depths of a major storm. In addition to being able to journal my heart out in anguish, and a newfound ability to express myself through poetry, I had a strong faith grounded in daily scripture reading and prayer, strong friendships with other spiritual friends, and a wisdom that comes from riding out other storms during my 70+ years.

This book is a summary of lessons in healing and self-discovery during the pandemic. It includes excerpts from my personal journal (formatted in italic type), blogs, links to pandemic selfie videos, several Facebook posts and scripts from Facebook Live episodes. You may notice that the "voice" in my blogs sounds like someone else wrote them when compared to my journal entries. The public persona of the blogs is me trying to be witty or helpful. My journal voice is at times troubled, wounded, angry and childish. But that's okay. Journaling is a vomit-on-the-page kind of activity and just who we are at that moment. Normally, journals are so private they're not shared for public consumption. But here I am showing my warts and my wants in hopes that you can see yourself and give yourself the liberty of finding the healing and hope that can come from journaling through your own storms.

Here's the disclaimer. This book presents a Christian's perspective and introspection on the pandemic and on extended family reactions and interactions. While it also includes references to scripture and prayer, it does not advocate a specific dogma or doctrine.

I suspect that readers will have experienced the positive and negative that are documented here in the context of getting through the enormous Covid-19 storms, storms that continue even now as we hear of new variations and outbreaks.

My humble prayer is that you will recognize yourself, your attitudes, and your love and connection to God and others as you wade through the mess of my life during the pandemic. May it help prepare you for our New Normal the way I hope writing all of this has prepared me.

Anne Spry

Life Before the Storm

"A bad thing can become a good thing if it's a God thing."–
Memoir class member Sylvia Morgan

Living on the Fringes of Frivolity

"You're worthless as teats on a boar hog."

Those words scalded their way into my family DNA and transformed me into an over-achieving adult. They're what I blame for my lack of emotional maturity, coupled with other childhood traumas that I could only deal with by stuffing them deep inside where, unbeknownst to me, they could do the most harm.

I think it was my mother who compared me to a boar hog. Or maybe my grandfather. I recently learned he had said the same thing to my cousins. And while my mother may not have said I was worthless, she made me feel I could do nothing right. I'd clean house and she'd come along and re-do the chores I'd just completed while harshly complaining of my ineptitude.

Now that I'm old and more mature, I know she was trying to muddle through her own insecurities–ones that originated with her hyper-critical, emotionally shut down, second-generation German father and a schizophrenic mother who suffered debilitating migraine headaches. I inherited the migraines, but not the schizophrenia, thank you, Jesus!

My dad was the son of the afore-mentioned boar hog insult hurler. A 5'7" Clark Gable-handsome man, he had drawn the short straw as dutiful slave to a driven Kansas farmer. Grandpa made the kids quit school in the eighth grade to help harvest and haul hay and to cover for him when he left Grandma with her nine kids so he could go to the local honky tonk.

By the time I was four and my brother was two, my dad was slowly pulling away from my grandfather, as were all the other slave-driven kids. Daddy had his own agricultural lime and trucking business, and we lived on 20 acres of alfalfa outside of Topeka, KS. Our life was enriched with cousins and extended family, and full of celebrations and mischief.

But that all stopped one August day in 1953 when my dad died in a trucking accident. That's when my mom went a little crazy, (thankfully not the schizophrenic kind.) But she had married even before she graduated from high school and given birth to me when she was only 18, so she deserves some slack. After Daddy died, Mother was determined to exert her independence and get away from the judgmental attitudes and prying eyes of those Kansas farm folks in the prudish 1950s.

We moved to Oklahoma and lived in a trailer court, beginning an odyssey that included new lovers and husbands for my mom and tons of trauma for everyone, especially me. At least that's what it felt like, after losing my dad, moving multiple times, being left with abusive babysitters (including the husband of one who molested me at age six when his wife left to go to the grocery store).

This is to give you some background on how messed up I was, just so you'll know how I could journal and write myself into healing, or a reasonable facsimile thereof. It took a long time and it's not all done – my life or my healing. Or my writing, for that matter.

My mother left *her* messed-up family to get married at age 18. I left *my* messed-up family to go to the University of Missouri and study journalism. Mother was smart, ambitious and creative but she could not afford to go to college or even finish high school. I could afford it, thanks to a trust fund set up with proceeds from a lawsuit by my dad's estate against the driver who hit him head-on and killed him.

Mizzou is where I met and married my first husband, winning a bonus jackpot in his close-knit Catholic family of 11 kids. Landing in that scenario was like falling into marshmallow fluff. The fun of family food fests and love was like a flash mob replacement for the extended family I left at age six to go live in a trailer court.

This doesn't mean I was instantly transported into self-acceptance after my childhood traumas, or that I completely ditched my old boar hog self. I still existed mostly on the fringes of frivolity. While my in-laws partied and joked all around me, went on vacations as one big happy group, watched or attended sporting events together, I stayed in a shy corner, reading a book or crocheting or otherwise trying to be productive and busy. But that was only after my husband and I returned from three plus years as Peace Corps volunteers in Brazil. It was also after we ran a café for a few years and after I went to work as an editor at my husband's hometown newspaper and finally got to use my journalism degree and training. It was also after we moved back to Columbia, MO for my husband to attend law school, which I helped put him through by working for a state agency and doing public relations/information work.

When we came back to my husband's hometown and he put out his law shingle on our soon-to-be renovated old brick home, I tried to do his secretarial work, but resented the hell out of it. I detested the drudgery of typing up wills, petitions, and other court documents, and longed to be using my creativity in writing investigative journalism pieces. Meanwhile, I was going to fertility doctors trying to get pregnant. The weekend I bought the local newspaper from a third-generation owner, I started hemorrhaging and lost my first pregnancy. Our son was born a year later and I wrote a personal column for the newspaper from the hospital. His cousin was born the next day to my sister-in-law, who was now typing my husband's court papers.

Six years later, after I helped campaign for his election as an associate circuit judge, my husband wanted a divorce. I got to keep the newspaper, but suddenly had to pay myself a wage after having operated the business for almost a decade as a hobby.

Within six months after the divorce papers were signed, my husband married our marriage counselor. Of course, I'm not gonna outline all the things I did or didn't do to contribute to the end of my first marriage. I was pretty messed up from childhood, remember? The failures were certainly not all in his court, pun intended.

I tried to learn my lessons, tried being single. But I just wanted to be loved and taken care of like the Prince Charming Cinderella bullshit we got fed as little girls in the fifties. So what do I do? Five years after the divorce I marry someone who was even more messed up than I was. Yup. I married a narcissist who was so threatened and jealous of my skills he took the psychological place of my critical mother. He tried to control me by managing my newspaper company's finances and operations. He drove customers away with his hot temper, childish tirades and petty jealousies. But he could work magic with money, moving it around and using credit cards for creative financing so he could buy a new car or two every year with company money.

But the man was a genius with computers and a skilled graphic artist. He kept the company up to date with software and hardware and did all our employee training. And he knew how to drive me up a wall just far enough, then turn on the charm and dial it down to make me forget why I was infuriated with him in the first place. In a true twist of irony, he was also gifted psychically and pushed me into a spirituality that I had never known in previous years of religious practices and church attendance.

His name was Marshall, just so you'll know when I refer to him later on. He was not healthy mentally or physically. We had moved to Kansas City, sold the newspaper to be closer to his family and to doctors, when he underwent a major hernia surgery and almost died on the operating table. He recovered, but his health was totally shot. I was giving him four insulin shots a day and I noticed his cognitive skills were decreasing. I took over bill paying and household management. I had previously taken over the care of his ailing stepmother, Rosie, who had developed dementia. I took groceries to her every week, and eventually filled out all the paperwork to qualify her for admission to a local nursing home in February of 2015. Immediately thereafter I went through her personal belongings and household items and parceled them out to family members and donated what was left to a local charity. Marshall was too ill to help physically. But we did go together to a funeral home to purchase a pre-need funeral plan for Rosie.

One day in July of 2015, after Marshall had already endured two emergency ambulance run hospital admissions for influenza, I drove him to the ER myself where we discovered he had an intestinal blockage. It couldn't be cleared, and doctors advised palliative care. He took his last breath when I was out of the room. First marriage: 21 years. Second marriage: 21 years. Third marriage: ongoing since 2018. And that's where this story begins.

Yes, I had tried the single life yet again, but I needed help keeping my power tools running. Seriously.

My first cousin Linda died of cancer a year and a day after my second husband died. Her husband, Wayne, and I had kept in touch and exchanged tips on all the paperwork and frustrations involved in the death of a spouse. On a whim, I called him one day to see if he wanted to come to Kansas City to help me celebrate my birthday at a local Brazilian barbecue restaurant. He came, and we enjoyed an afternoon together. It was a good break from death paperwork.

Then came the day I couldn't get my weed whacker started and my self-propelled lawnmower was sputtering. I called Wayne to see if he could troubleshoot them. He is a wizard at fixing things and got both running. After that, we talked on the phone for hours several nights a week. He then began driving back and forth on weekends to help with landscaping projects at my house in Kansas City. Soon we were talking about making our relationship permanent, but when his daughter and son-in-law began looking for a place to live that was closer to an employer, my house seemed a perfect solution. They moved in after I moved out, and by October of 2018, Wayne and I were married.

Now you have some of the cast of characters and the timeline of my numerous dysfunctions and life backstories. You're up to speed on the who, what, when, where and why. All that's left now is to uncover the how–how I journaled and wrote myself out of the universal storm that began in March of 2020.

Saying Goodbye to My Home

June 20, 2018

Goodbye house. Goodbye trees. Goodbye shed with your window-box marigolds and the strawberry bed that I left for the chipmunks. Goodbye deck where I set up my hammock and watched the clouds. Goodbye back porch where I prayed and sometimes bawled.

This is the quietest this house has been since August of 2011. Or was it July when Marshall and I moved in? It was hot enough to fry the air conditioner and cause us to have to stay overnight elsewhere. This house has been such a haven of peace and quiet beauty but I'm sure I will find that and make that with Wayne.

Life always changes as new chapters begin. I can't be like Lot's wife and keep looking back or I'll turn to stone...or was it salt? In place of this place, I go to my old/new home, the place where my life began–my family and ancestral home.

I led the moving van last Thursday in my mini-van packed to the roof with what the movers couldn't shove in their truck. My two dogs and a squalling cat were with me. I was a mile from my new house, approaching the turnoff to my new street, when the car filled with the intoxicating scent of freshly cut alfalfa. I breathed it in deeply, then scanned the landscape for the field, or any sign of a tractor cutting hay. But there was no alfalfa field, no tractor. I took that wonderful smell as a "welcome home" from my long-deceased father. It was a precious reminder of the time in my childhood that I had steered a hay truck at age four while he and his brothers loaded hay onto the truck bed.

August 25, 2018

What a beautiful scene I get to look at from the window of my dressing room! The cumulus clouds are painting a picture as they billow above the distant tree line that rises above newly green pastures. We've been blessed with a few drought-busting rains that caused the basement sump pump to kick on for the first time in nine months. So much is going on in our lives right now and I've not been faithful about journaling.

September 8, 2018

A string of gloomy, gray days has increased my lethargy lately. I'm restless, unsettled and wondering if I made a mistake in re-locating here. It's not that I don't love Wayne. I just feel a bit isolated, disconnected, and disoriented. I even feel a little disconnected from God and I can't seem to get a morning prayer and meditation routine established.

At Wayne's urging, I've tried to back off from pushing myself so hard. But I do find great satisfaction in my work. Yesterday I began organizing book client Joseph Matovu's memoir, cutting and pasting segments of interview notes into the beginnings of chapters. I became acquainted with Joseph at the church I attended in Kansas City. He was in a wheelchair and I became intrigued by his heavy British accent when he did scripture readings. I soon learned that he became paralyzed from the waist down in a farming accident in Wamego, KS, when he came from Africa to the states to study. He had planned to return to Uganda to teach but his accident resulted in his permanent residency in Kansas City. He went on to become the first paralyzed person to graduate from Rockhurst College, then became one of the driving forces in the disabilities movement in Kansas City, petitioning city government to install handicapped access in city buildings and on city sidewalks.

I conducted many interviews with Joseph to get his story recorded for a memoir. After moving away, I worried that we would not be able to continue our collaboration but now I've taken it up again. I began with stories of his early life and began editing, finessing and adding transitions to the narrative. I was struck by one of his comments in an interview. He said, "You are downloading me and causing the memories to come out – things I had totally forgotten." Comments like that keep me motivated and on track with my purpose.

Friday, October 12, 2018

Today is our wedding day. It doesn't seem much different than any other day. Our pastor said it would be unusual if neither of us felt any jitters of trepidation. We don't think we will. We know each other. We accept each other's weaknesses and faults. Maybe we'd have jitters if we were having a church full of witnesses, of family and friends. But some of Wayne's relatives do not approve of our marriage so soon after Linda died. This private ceremony takes care of our concerns over their disapproval. At least we don't have to confront it this way. It's going to be just the minister, us and two witnesses.

Our marriage in a church is a sign and symbol that we are grounded in faith and seeking God's blessing. We are acknowledging to Him our gratitude for bringing us together late in life, as we lift each other up, and prepare ourselves for any spiritual battles we may have to face. We know where our strength comes from. And now we can more securely face what lies ahead. Now we can continue building our future with God as our foundation and strength.

November 17, 2018

I woke up from a dream this morning almost in tears because I couldn't do a flip. Everyone else in my class had executed one. I whined to the instructor that I had always been able to do cartwheels, but attempting a flip gave me vertigo due to some inner ear problems. I kept trying, still fearful of landing on the hardwood floor. My bones kept creaking and popping. When I woke up my first thought was, "Good God! You're 69 years old – way too old to do a flip!"

This dream must be showing me my subconscious fears in attempting to start a new career as a book publisher so late in life. Or maybe it's more literal, and I'm confronting some actual physical limitations.

Wayne will be gone all morning working cattle. There are so many things I'd like to do today and need to do, like dusting, which I hate. I'm still getting settled into this house. But here is a list of other things I could and should do: My jewelry project box, hang a few pictures, bring the antique secretary upstairs, clear off the display case to use for holiday displays, bring out the Thanksgiving stuff, work on three clients' books and prepare for Monday's memoir class.

February 15, 2019

In the last few days I've begun writing a very personal, spiritually focused memoir. It's really sparking some painful memories and causing disturbing dreams, like the one about trying to do flips.

February 16, 2019

I found two of my father's diaries yesterday. I was searching for journals I had done as a young woman to help me fill in the blanks of those years.

While looking at my dad's diaries just now, I had a flashback to when Mother gave them to me. I don't know the year, but I can see her opening that blonde-finished cedar chest and pulling them out. I'm so amazed that she kept them. She also pulled out some of my baby clothes and my dad's pipe. I have them now and plan to make a shadow box display.

I hope I can adequately connect my own history and personal artifacts with my family's and my ancestors'.

Blog

A Bad Thing Can Become a Good Thing If It's a God Thing

February 25, 2019 – There is always a ray of sunshine somewhere that will make the storms bearable. At least that's what the members of my memoir group are teaching me.

As we sat around the table yesterday in my church's fellowship hall, listening to some amazing stories of courage and perseverance, a feeling of deep humility and gratitude came over me. In my organizing and facilitating of another memoir group (one of three so far) it occurred to me that I was the one gaining the rewards and benefits of this form of storytelling.

The members of this group come together each month to learn how to preserve the stories of their lives so they can hand them down to their children and grandchildren and other family members. I give them assignments and we do some in-class writing. My role is easy. But they dig deep into their souls and find the stories that hold the deepest and most legacy-bearing lessons.

One woman read her story of how she got through a serious surgery and had to endure– perhaps for the first time ever–a loss of control over her future. She put her life in the hands of a surgeon, overcoming fears of the risks and potentially adverse outcomes, and finally gave it all up to prayer and trust. Another class member shared briefly how her family got a glimpse of Heaven in the eyes and words of her dying mother.

Another class member told us about almost losing her life to a debilitating disease, sharing the Bible passages, the hymns and the miracles that had saved her. One of those was "It Is Well With My Soul," which our choir had just sung at Sunday's service. As this woman shared a story of intense pain, she said she had just begun realizing how many other side stories fed into this one. And one of those stories highlighted the fast friendship that grew out of her hospital encounter with an IV therapist, a woman who now sat at the table with the rest of us and had encouraged her to join this class. As she explained succinctly in a quote I had to capture in my notebook, "A bad thing can become a good thing if it's a God thing."

Yet another class member gave us a glimpse into the revelations she gained by having an anxiety attack at age 60, and how she was able to later help a young man going through the same experience.

The people in my memoir class have all reached an age where soul stories matter. We hope to see it as the "age of wisdom." It's a time when we may find ourselves looking back more than we look forward. Not that we're stuck in the past. But now we can take the time to see what our life experiences have taught us. As I looked around the table yesterday, I again marveled at how each person's story carries lessons for others who may yet endure similar challenges. These individuals are taking their life parables a step further than most of us. They are recording theirs, making them accessible to their family and maybe even the world at large. What is priceless about every single one of them is that they always end up giving God the glory. In coming home to their soul stories, through the power of the written or spoken word, they are giving credit to the original author of life.

Children Are Models of Purity and Innocence

March 2, 2019

I love today's scripture reading from the website Laudate. I continue to use this Catholic resource in my daily meditation and prayer time, even though I'm no longer attending Mass and have joined the Presbyterian Church that my family has attended for generations.

In the reading, Jesus rebuked his disciples when they tried to keep the children from bugging Him. So many thoughts and memories came flooding into my head from that reading. I have such an affinity and love for little children. It may be my imagination, but we always seem drawn to each other out in public, even total strangers, and always exchange smiles. It has to be the spirit of God that draws us to each other. They are still so pure of heart and such innocent creatures. Perhaps I am seeing in them some semblance of my own lost innocence.

The other thing that came to mind in the reading was the children I encountered in Brazil and their beautiful custom of coming up to me with their hands upturned and saying, "Abença titia" or "Bless me, Auntie." At that point it was customary to put my hand on their heads and say, "God bless you, my child." This quaint but beautiful custom has the adult playing the role of Christ. If only that simple blessing could preserve their innocence and simplicity for the rest of their lives.

March 11, 2019

I wish I could recapture the sentiments of a heartfelt prayer last Wednesday while on the way to Kansas City. I had suddenly remembered what Fr. Lockwood, the priest in the church I attended while living in the city, said about the history of mankind being the history of God. So, our own history is God's story, with Him working in and through us to manifest his divine plan. And when we look back at it and record it, that helps us to see the over-arching design and beautiful simplicity of it. We can see our sins and mistakes and trials as a perfecting process on the road to holiness.

Jumping into Volunteer, Creative Activities

The remainder of 2019 saw me jumping into volunteer organizations as a way to make friends and explore creative pursuits in my new home. I joined a Sweet Adelines group and began learning to sing barbershop harmony music. I was asked by a friend I had written grants for in Kansas City to serve as a board member for an organization he had just joined as executive director. The organization served clients with mental health issues and offered a clubhouse that served daily meals and a place to play games, do laundry and shower. It also offered residential housing to qualified individuals.

I also joined the Kansas Authors Club and attended meetings once a month at Topeka's wonderful public library.

In late March I joined my business partner, Cheri, in a trip to Nauvoo, IL, to present a program on personal history.

In late June of 2019 I returned to Kansas City for a book launch. I had been collaborating with the daughter of a woman who disappeared several years ago while doing door-to-door marketing in Independence, MO. Her dismembered body was eventually discovered in a muddy riverbank and a suspect was charged and tried for her murder. The book, ***Searching for Summer: A Solved but Unresolved Missing Persons Case,*** was co-authored with Brandy Shipp Rogge to capture the memory of her mother as more than a murder victim. Brandy and I then had a local author event at the Independence Barnes and Noble store following the successful June book launch. It was an intense experience just getting the book published, as it was only the second jacketed hardcover book I had formatted and published.

I continued to drive to Kansas City once a week to babysit my grandchildren and celebrated my 70th birthday at home with family. In October, I helped an overseas client publish and promote a unique book that was a graphic "novel." The book's cartoons highlighted the wit and wisdom of the author's mother, who was a nursing home resident. The author and illustrator both live in Africa and came to Kansas City for the book launch at Prospero's Bookstore in Kansas City, KS, and appeared on a TV interview I set up for them.

The year ended with another big birthday celebration, as my husband turned 70 the day after Christmas. His kids and grandkids surprised him with a big dinner at the local Red Lobster, then we came back to the house for a "This is Your Life" slideshow, cake and ice cream.

It was a gratifying if intense year for both of us. I loved the life we were building together, and enjoyed regular contact with my father's family members. Two aunts and an uncle lived nearby, as did several cousins. And I especially loved my babysitting gigs in Kansas City. My favorite activity was reading to them.

All the interaction I enjoyed with family and friends–all the activity with volunteer organizations, all the trips to the city to babysit–all that was about to end abruptly.

Signing copies of the book, "Searching for Summer" in July, 2019.

Discovering Quilting

Quilting became my thing in early 2020. In settling into our home I had run across stacks of t-shirts and uniform shirts my husband had acquired during his military career. My friend, Helen, knew a gifted quilter named Diane. I took the shirts to her. It wasn't long before we had a finished product. My husband was quite pleased.

Having one quilt completed gave me the courage to tackle a project my mother had begun decades ago–a king sized, cross-stitched quilt top. When I acquired the project at her death, the embroidered top was less than half finished. It took me another decade to finish the cross-stitching. Diane took it from there.

My dog Ro-Ro 'helping' me embroider

The finished king size quilt

The Storm Hits

You may not control all the events that happen to you, but you can decide not to be reduced by them. *–Maya Angelou*

Journaling Through the First Days

Business closures, lockdowns, self-quarantines and social distancing were new terms added to the 2020 world lexicon. We also learned about supply chain disruptions, as we faced empty store shelves.

March 19, 2020

This self-quarantining and social distancing seems to be whispering urgently in my ear to get things done, to make things right, to prepare for the beginning of the end. Instead, like a deer caught in the headlights, I float mechanically, just going through the motions.

I find myself torn between checking on Facebook to stay in touch with friends and cleaning; between wanting to downsize and sanitize; between doing my own writing projects and working on client projects; between craft projects and home décor, between baking bread and wanting to plant early vegetables; between learning hydroponics and podcasting. I'm left wondering how to establish a new routine.

March 25, 2020

As I was reading today's reflections on scripture and on the signs God has given us, it occurred to me that this pandemic is certainly a sign–a big sign calling us to come back to God, to turn inward, to focus on our families and friends and on the only thing that lasts–God's love and our own love for each other.

March 27, 2020

In prayer and meditation this morning, I was impressed to hasten the spread of my storytelling mission. As I look at the Kansas map showing the gradual spread westward of this pandemic, it struck me fully that this is a supernatural thing. And yesterday it struck me that we are re-living the Passover. We are inside our homes waiting for the Angel of Death to pass over us, praying that he spares us and our loved ones. We don't have our lintels painted with the blood of the Lamb, but if our hearts are filled with the Spirit, with the love of God, surely death at this time will pass us by.

My Best Friend's Husband Dies

March 28, 2020

When my phone rang at 6:00 this morning, I wondered why Wayne had set his alarm. I was not awake enough to realize it was my own ringtone. When I looked at the caller ID, I was filled with dread.

"Chris and George."

I fumbled around, then hit the return call button when I couldn't manage to answer the call in time. I still had my CPAP mask on. Finally, I was able to get Chris on the line and learned that George had passed early this morning. She wanted me to give the news to our high school friends, all the girls who had managed to get together for lunch at least once a year since we graduated.

Later, in my morning prayers, I thanked God for giving Chris her once-in-a-lifetime, late-life love. It is so difficult to understand why George was taken away so soon. Especially when he was such a loving, selfless servant to so many. And why now, when we are in quarantine and Chris can only accept the comforts of her immediate family? As her friend, I can't be with her and give her a hug or cry with her.

My morning prayers weren't as heartfelt today. The connection was clouded by my distracted thoughts and my perpetual need to understand the ways of God, the whys of God. Like the perpetual reporter I will always be, I want to interview Him, call Him to task for his ruling. I know that death is our ultimate end, but I also know we are destined for eternal life in His light. Our souls will go on and the loved ones we lose are still with us. If only we could access our abilities to feel them and communicate with them and see them.

March 31, 2020

Yesterday I acted quickly on the prompting I had during prayer. I recorded three videos in quick succession. They are unpolished but heartfelt. I was surprised at how easy it was to do.

If we are all living online now, from teachers to chorus groups to officials using social media to give news updates on the virus, it's finally

Riding Rainbows Through the Storms

time for me to get with the program. I need to share my purpose with a virtual audience and show and tell why it is so important, now more than ever, to preserve our stories. We need to use this time of the pandemic to gather the teaching stories of our lives, in the same way that Jesus left us his parables in the pages of the most important history ever written. In the same way that the Bible is the history of God's people, given to us as a gift and a guide, our own history should be left to our families, full of personal parables that will instruct our children, grandchildren, friends and even our enemies.

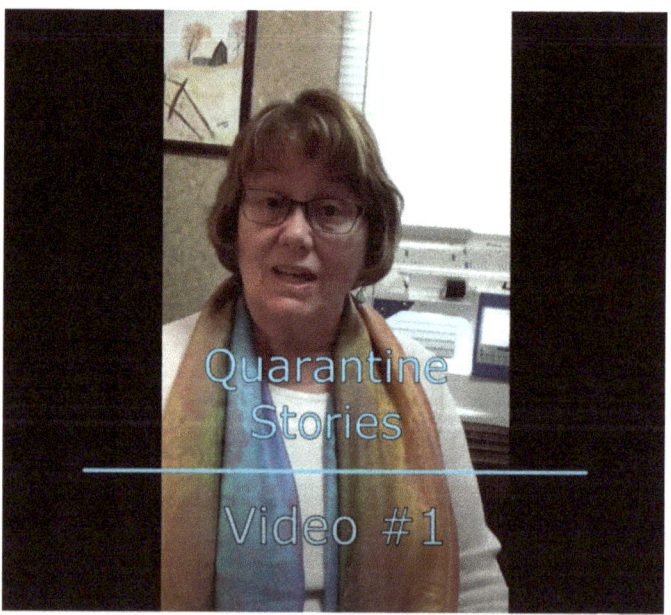

https://tinyurl.com/IntroducingQuarantineStories

The wall plaque I started Sunday in a manic frenzy of creativity. Only slightly ironic, since we can't "Gather Together" right now.

Blog

Thank You, Hobby Lobby, for Staying Open

The words on the Facebook post immediately caused my blood to boil. A progressive website smeared the CEO of Hobby Lobby as stupid and irresponsible for deciding to keep his stores open in states where he has not been ordered to shut down.

The blog on this website also ridiculed the Christian-owned company for founder David Green's letter to employees last week. In addition to citing the measures the stores would implement to keep employees and customers safe, Green said his wife, Barbara, the family's "prayer warrior," had three words put on her heart by God during prayer. Those three words: Guide, Guard and Groom.

As the letter explained, "We serve a God who will guide us through this storm, who will guard us as we travel to places never seen before, and who, as a result of this experience, will groom us to be better than we could have ever thought possible before now."

Yarn and glitter are good, don't they know?

Another comment from friendlyatheist.com: "Unlike grocery stores, it's hard to make the case that yarn and glitter are essential products in a time of crisis."

Oh, but they are! Yarn and glitter and scrapbook supplies and paints and sewing supplies are indeed essential during these days of social isolation and anxiety. Just as office supplies are now more important than ever while so many of us work from home.

In fact, art supplies are such a crucial part of so many lives that a local mental health institution has put together client coping kits that contain them. The staff has even compiled suggestions for clients to make their own kits. They could include paper, crayons and markers, paints, pre-made design templates for coloring, old magazines or newspapers for cutting out words or phrases for collages, and, of course, household glue. I bet that glitter and yarn would also be good elements for a coping kit.

Beware the manic woman lost in the art aisles

Since this worldwide crisis began, and since my scheduling calendar is suddenly bereft of appointments and deadlines, I have behaved like a manic Ever Ready Bunny lost in an art supplies store like Hobby Lobby. These days I have no excuse for putting my arts and crafts projects and unfinished home décor plans on the back burner.

Matter of fact, my husband expressed some mild alarm yesterday at my level of crafty multi-tasking. He watched me start embroidering a little wall plaque with the words "Gather Together." Ironic now, isn't it, since we can't gather anymore? I put it aside for a bit and hauled out the color-coordinated hoard of neckties left behind by my deceased second husband and began weaving them together to cover the faded cushions of a rocker in the living room. I also wove the red and white gingham ribbon purchased weeks ago into the wire slats of the kitchen pantry shelves, embellishing the kitchen with an additional spot of country décor already present in curtains.

The expired food items need clearing out

When the stay-at-home suggestions first blasted from multiple televised news conferences, I also went into a frenzy of baking and cooking. My intuition (God, maybe?) told me the freezers needed to be cleared of nearly expired foods so they wouldn't go to waste.

My husband's reaction to discovering that the meatball package slowly taking on air on the top shelf of the freezer had morphed into barbecue sliders in the crockpot? At first, skepticism, then raised eyebrows, just before the first taste. But he pronounced them good. Whew!

However, my use of the remaining off-brand Spanish peanuts and the holiday chocolate bark in

My unfinished necktie chair, put together right now with loose weaving on the bottom and basting stitches on the upright cushion. If I can keep the cat off of it, it might get finished during social isolation productivity.

We will discover shortly just how much red and white gingham is overkill.

the pantry that was starting to take on that expired-looking white coating to make peanut clusters, didn't produce a report card of A. Maybe a C+. He only eats them because no other sweets have materialized from the social isolation kitchen...yet. But, oh, the plans I have!

The hills are alive with red gingham

Maybe I should warn him that I have watched Julie Andrews in *Sound of Music* many times and may find new uses for our curtains during this frenzy of creativity.

Unlike the atheist skeptics, I do believe that God especially touches our hearts during times of crisis, whether we are retirees or company CEOs, housewives or minimum wage retail workers. Even the *Wall Street Journal* opinion column yesterday noted that this time of fear, anxiety and social isolation could be meant to help us get our priorities straight. Ironically, I see it as a time when we can better connect with each other and our own souls. Now we have the free time to get uncover our expressive needs through art, writing and music. We can talk to God or the walls or our fellow isolation inmates more often and on a deeper level. We can stay in touch with friends and family. We can pray more often, or perhaps for the first time. We can love ourselves and each other and find imaginative ways to do so, minus the important sense of touch through hugs. We can channel our energies into creative projects while we learn to send healing and hopeful energy waves to our loved ones on FaceTime.

We can do this, my fellow manic bunnies.

Blog:

Birthing Quarantine Stories
as a Coping Strategy

These are anxious days. We read or watch the grim daily Covid-19 statistics. Then we spend sleepless nights anticipating things that could go wrong in our households, with our families and friends.

How about, instead of all the worrying, we take advantage of the Pause button the universe handed us? Why not take this time to record our personal stories from this unique 2020 timeline as we witness dramatic, profound events nearly every day?

Personal Chapters wants to help you take advantage of this time by recording your part in current history. Record it in writing in a journal. Record it in selfies or videos. Sing out your soul and your stress. Record it on a voice recording app. You are creative. You are unique.

We'll figuratively hold your hand and guide you. When the quarantine and social distancing finally lift, Personal Chapters will have some chances to hold your hand in person. Maybe even give you a hug in the flesh!

(Read on to discover how that played out.)

It was one of those epic fails

I was just trying to encourage people to start recording their personal history as a pandemic priority.

After I pushed the publish button on the first YouTube video of Quarantine Stories, I watched it in the actual platform.

Sad. Melancholy. And that's exactly what a friend observed when I asked for her feedback.

In that first episode I whined about not being able to see my grandkids or hug my friends. I didn't smile enough. Heck, even my intro music sounded sad.

In short, that first attempt at becoming a YouTube star (not really my true aspiration) showed the personality of a melancholy crybaby.

But it made me admit I've been a melancholic my whole life. I've been so serious and sad for just shy of 70 years that one of my friends named a cow after me. It had sad brown eyes just like mine.

My first foray into YouTube videos made me realize the only times in my life I haven't been dead-serious-sad is when I was eating something sweet or writing.

Yet my critiquing friend thinks I'm funny. Just because she always laughed out loud at the personal columns I wrote for my newspaper.

Enough about my sense of humor, or lack thereof. The question here is: How am I going to encourage and inspire you all to write down your memories and life stories while we're all on pandemic house arrest? I realize my friend had it right when she told me that people won't respond to melancholy.

No. We get through the tough times by finding some fun and funnies. And through poking fun at ourselves.

My stepson Dana has been so bored during this pandemic that he recorded two desperate short videos and took a silly selfie. But then, he has never been serious in his life. I tell him frequently that he missed his calling. Instead of being a helicopter mechanic, he should have been a standup comic or a singer. He has a beautiful, melt-your-heart voice. Every time he sings at a family gathering or party, someone has the foresight to record a video.

Now, with these goofy selfie videos and his music videos, Dana has a great start on his personal history. If nothing else, there will be lots of material to pull from for his funeral service. More importantly, his daughters and grandchildren will have visual reminders of his sense of humor and the vital force that animates

Dana and his silly pandemic selfie.

his soul.

How about you? What are you doing to entertain yourself while under stay-at-home orders? How do you cope? Do you stay in your pajamas all day? What things do you find on Facebook feeds that are hilarious? Are you a future standup comic like Dana, or a depressing melancholic like me?

Channel all that boredom

How are you using this time of social distancing? Are you up to the challenge of learning how to channel your boredom and energies into learning something about yourselOr into building a legacy of memories into something your family can hold onto when you're gone?

Last week my son Michael conquered his pandemic boredom by building a wooden hammock stand from plans he snagged on the Internet. How are you coping with boredom?

Let me help you with this

Bottom line? I want to help you with practical suggestions about how to get through this scary time so you'll have something concrete when we come out of it. I'll do my best to keep things light. I'll try to make you laugh or at least chuckle.

This is going to be fun, said the melancholic.

My son, Michael's pandemic project hammock stand.

Subsequent Attempts at YouTube Stardom

https://tinyurl.com/TheWisdomofElders

https://tinyurl.com/FindingTheHumorInToughTimes

Adapting to Storm Conditions

"Every soul has to withstand great pressure and to be well tested." –The Quiet Mind: Sayings of White Eagle, ©*The White Eagle Lodge, used with permission.*

Riding Rainbows Through the Storms

Learning the Elements of Self Care

Saturday, April 11, 2020

I learned something about myself through fasting yesterday. I was totally self-critical, thinking I wasn't doing it the right way. And I caught myself just grabbing or reaching for a snack. Apparently, I graze all day without even being aware of it. But today I feel lighter in many ways, including emotionally and physically. I'm more energetic. I read this morning in my little White Eagle book* that if we don't take care of ourselves properly, we continually slay the God within us.

April 18, 2020

Quarantine Quote: Humanity will not be converted by the distressed. *This came from today's reflections on the scriptures. Immediately my mind went to using this quote as a springboard for a blog, making it about all the things that staying home during the pandemic has done for us:*

• *Our meals at home*

• *Our cleaning and creativity as we made our homes even better sanctuaries.*

• *Our new sense with our spouses and families that we're in this together and more of a unified, protective and proactive team.*

• *Our attempts to even make our homes places of worship and meditation.*

• *Our recognition that we have not been good stewards of the earth as we see pollution diminish.*

• *And how about how we've reconnected with our own souls? I sure have.*

I tried to have a FaceTime call with Rosie at the nursing home yesterday but she did not recognize me or my voice, or even the iPhone the nurse's aid was holding in front of her. Her dementia has really

---

* *The Quiet Mind: Sayings of White Eagle*, The White Eagle Publishing Trust, Hampshire, England, 1972, reprinted 2017. Used with permission worsened. *I assume the purpose for all these negatives is for us to recognize and extend a helping hand to all those "least of these" people that we can't ignore so much anymore. We hear their cries now more than ever and long to rush to their sides to assist. Because we are them and they are us.*

April 21, 2020

I finished the necktie chair cushion project. Practiced my music, finally. Then had a fast-paced Zoom meeting and rehearsal. Zoom would even be a good platform to collaborate with my book client, Theresa.

April 24, 2020

My whole life has been like a test of the emergency broadcast system. And for most of my life, I have failed the test.

I've been quiet this week. No blogs, no videos. Not because I have nothing to say or give. Maybe it's because I'm regrouping and regathering strength for a fresh surge of energy and activity. I've been more focused on home and hearth, from trying to reorganize the garage and office, to putting a beautiful basket of silk flowers on the hearth; from installing new software on my computer to bringing in more light for my desk.

April 25, 2020

I have been in so much mental turmoil this week. Not sure why, except that this quarantine seems endless. Yesterday we had to go out and pick up a gift for my granddaughter from Target. It did lift my spirits to get out. But yesterday I realized that our lives–our world– has changed and will never go back to the way it was before the pandemic.

I hope it has helped me rely more on God, to deepen my relationship with Him. It has certainly made me realize how messed up I can get without turning to Him in prayer. Yesterday's storm and brief power outage showed me that. When I couldn't get my new computer re-started, I lost it. Cussed. Almost cried. Then I realized, once again, I hadn't yet prayed. Things always go more smoothly when I start the day with prayer.

Blog:
Some Candid Covid Comments

I've been scaring myself into the middle of next year. All it took was reading speculations in the press about new realities facing us as the economy begins to open up.

Here's what frightens me:
• No spectator sports in big stadiums.
•Colleges and universities gravitating to online classes entirely.
• Social distancing for the rest of our lives.
• Stores and eateries taking your temperature before allowing you to go through their doors.
• Wearing a mask in public all the time.

That last prediction bothers me more than any of the others. On my last few grocery/prescription runs, wearing something over my mouth (can they make up their }%^* minds whether it's for our own or everyone else's protection?!) left me with a bad taste.

My N95 mask made me feel guilty, certain I would be arrested by mask cops for using something that should be reserved for doctors and nurses. However, I would have to tell the arresting officer I retrieved it from our basement, where it had been stored since 2016, left behind by my cousin's hospice nurses. I couldn't find an expiration date, but it sure smells bad, like maybe it was folded on the floor of a sweatshop in a third world country. Or maybe the smell is just basement B. O. mixed with my bad breath.

Anyway, the N95 fogged

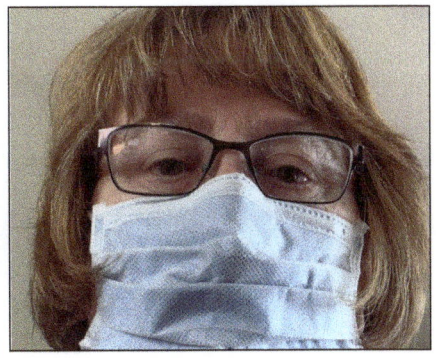

Mask 1-The N95

up my glasses and made me hyperventilate.

When I ran out today, I debated which mask to wear...the used N95, a pretty little mask a book client sent in the mail or a scarf that matched my top. I have a thing about color coordination. Just ask my friends. They think I always look like I am ready for a photo shoot—jewelry perfectly mated with clothing. In keeping up that dubious facade, I decided to color coordinate today's trip out of the house.

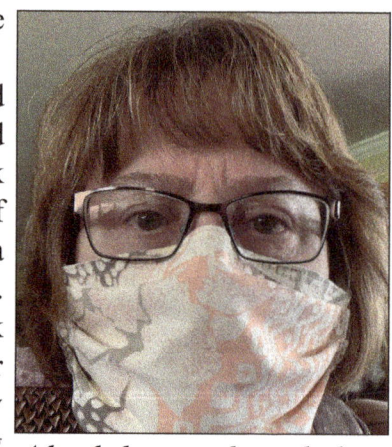

A lovely homemade mask given to me by a book client who loves to sew.

This attempt to make a fashion statement while complying with citizen PPE protocols failed miserably.

I could never get the hang of all those scarf tying videos that circulated years ago. All I ever managed was a big, balled-up knot in the center of my chest. Never succeeded with a graceful drape of any kind. Especially not today.

I tried tying the scarf behind my head. To one side. To the back. It kept sliding down my short nose. Every time I put it back up there, I wondered what that hand had just touched, and if I could last without being contaminated until I got to the hand sanitizer in the car. And wondered if it's safe to use hand sanitizer on your face.

Future fashion statement? Maybe I could hang my color coordinated earrings from the clips?

Then wondered how cool it would be to keep a scarf in place with potato chip clips.

Here are two more observations gleaned from today's grocery outing:

1. Just when you put mask in place and head for the store doors is the exact moment your nose needs scratching.

2. OMG, is that how bad my breath smells all the time?

By the time I finally got out of the store, after several brushes with potential social distancing death, I knew with total certainty the absolute best use for my scarf/ mask.

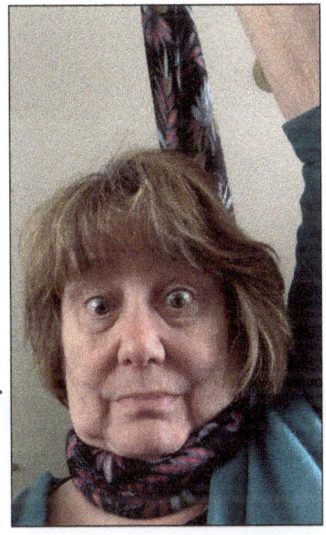

Does this scarf turned mask turned noose make my face look too fat?

P.S. Forgot a few things

1. As someone who has a lifetime habit of looking at everyone's mouth and teeth while they talk, I see the permanent use of masks in social settings as impending disaster. Maybe I should wear my hearing aids in public, because watching someone's lips has always been insurance that I can decipher what they're saying. And no, it is not a personality defect that I can't look you in the eye.

2. My iPhone does not recognize me in a mask.

3. My husband does not recognize a military friend in Walmart until the guy is already speed-walking down the next aisle.

Got the Pandemic Blues?
Rediscover Music

What does music do for you? During this time of quarantines and social distancing, call on music to get you through the dark days.

I've finally learned that we're all born with the capacity to sing. We start life with a love of music. We surely listened to choirs of angels in our pre-mortal lives. Once we're born, I think we spend a lot of time searching for that same heavenly sound.

Sometimes our music dies...

For too many of us, our love of music dies an early death.

For me, it started to die after some traumatic childhood experiences. It died almost completely when I was told to shut up. That I couldn't carry a tune in a bucket. Well, I *was* singing the **Star-Spangled Banner** from the back seat on a family trip. At the top of my lungs.

I didn't rediscover music until decades later. I started singing in a church choir after my second husband died. I still sing in a church choir, or at least I did before this pandemic. Now I sing with a Sweet Adelines group.

...but it's never too late to rediscover it

I hope you will think about using this time of staying cooped up at home to rediscover your music mojo.

Here are some suggestions on how to get your music mojo on:

• Dance to a favorite tune while you disinfect doorknobs and light switches.

• Play oldies on your stereo or a favorite radio station while you work from home. Sing along too, if your boss lets you get away with that.

• Old childhood favorites like *"Itsy Bitsy Spider"* are always a good bet while you're on a FaceTime call with the grandkids.

• Hum a favorite hymn while you're looking out the window or while washing your hands for the umpteenth time.

• Act as if you can scream away this danged virus. Jam on your air guitar while you listen to AC/DC play *"Thunderstruck."*

• If you can't stand your singing voice, use your listening ears or your video eyes and call up all your favs on YouTube.

• This might be the time to pick up the guitar that's been gathering dust in a corner. Again, check out all the YouTube videos that will teach you how to play. If you don't have a guitar, play a kazoo, or that mini steel drum someone got you for Christmas or a birthday. Remember how, as a kid, you put waxed paper over a comb and made your own kazoo? Do that again.

Music lets you access emotions

When I suffered some early childhood traumas, I used the typical defense mechanism–not letting anyone see what I was feeling. I stuffed emotion down deep. I built a brick wall around my heart. Then I didn't let love in or out.

I could only let my feelings show on paper. I confided to my diaries and journals. But music could always bring the emotions up and out. Music could always move me to tears.

Decades ago, I bought a spinet piano, making $25 a month payments until it was finally mine. Then, anytime I felt depressed or restless, I sat at the piano and pounded out my feelings. I played until my shoulders got stiff and I was totally worn out.

These days I play the piano when I'm happy. I even conquered my self-consciousness and can play in front of my husband. He has never criticized what or how I play. He plays the guitar, and I never criticize him either.

Find your own singing voice or your own ability to play some kind of instrument. Compose your own *Etude on a Pandemic*

Theme. Then help your children and grandchildren find their voices and their own love of music.

Music is one of the most valuable legacies we can leave our families. The world needs your music now more than ever.

Our local Sweet Adelines group stayed connected and focused on our music during the pandemic by holding Zoom rehearsals and classes. We continued practicing our singing in these sessions by muting our microphones and singing in our own space until the day we could finally gather in person again.

Blog:
Pandemic Positivity–A Candle in the Window, a Bear on the Porch

Although I retired from it in 2011, I am so proud of the Fourth Estate.

The Easter Monday edition of the local newspaper carried so many positive affirmations designed to dispel the gloom of this pandemic, it spurred me to join the campaign.

• A feature story detailed the efforts of a Garden City, Kansas mother to create some pandemic fun by starting a local bear hunt. The Facebook page she created urged friends and neighbors to put a stuffed bear on their front porches, so that when families go for walks, they can spot the bears and report the sightings. What fun!

• A columnist today urged everyone to put a battery-operated candle in a window of the house in a sign of solidarity, in a similar gesture that some of us exercised by turning off our front porch lights to conserve energy during the crisis of the 1980s.

• An advice columnist applauded the efforts of a couple that was financially assisting the immigrant family next door. The couple could afford it and wanted to help without hurting the immigrants' pride.

• Finally, the lead editorial called on all of us to consider how we are adhering to stay-at-home orders and doing our part in other ways to "flatten the curve" of Covid-19 infections. What will we tell our children or grandchildren years after this is over? Did we set a good example?

From the beginning of this crisis, newspapers and broadcast news channels began an auto-respond reaction, with little thought to covering the bottom line. Like when *The Wall Street Journal* and other national publications began offering their practical tips and news updates from in front of a pay wall instead of behind one.

Like when local TV news anchors repeated the symptoms of this virus with every broadcast. Like when local newspapers started filling up former advertising space with messages of positivity and hope seasoned with practical coping tips. This was, and is now ,journalism at its best.

And just as we have no idea how we all will emerge from this pandemic war with its massive unemployment and mass burials, we have no idea how the Fourth Estate will ultimately emerge on the other side of all this. But I salute my former colleagues in small towns and urban areas. I applaud those who were still trying to eke out a living when all this came crashing down around them, closing businesses they rely on for advertising. I pray for their survival and thank them for their service.

Words matter now more than ever. The words of these faithful news outlets have influenced at least one person. And that could be enough to start a tsunami of positivity.

Now, if you'll excuse me, I have to go put a bear on my front porch and a candle in my window.

Blog:

Trying out old recipes to honor a relative on hospice care

Burnt Sugar Cake earned my Aunt Gene several blue ribbons at local fairs. This was in the 1950s when cooking and gardening skills could give you bragging rights and a covey of green-eyed-jealous enemies. Some of her recipes were family secrets for years. Until they weren't. Until they appeared in a church cookbook.

The courage to try new-old skill sets

My dear departed cousin Linda collected cookbooks. When I came into her house as the beneficiary of her husband and a mountain of knick-knacks and what-nots, it became my job to sort through that collection and disperse them to her daughters and stepdaughters. I kept a few for myself, especially a spattered old blue thing called *Community Favorites II: Compiled by Wakarusa Presbyterian Church, Wakarusa, Kansas.*

The best way to come into these church cookbooks is through inheritance. I have my mother's cookbook from one of the Lutheran churches she attended. Also have one from the Hamilton, Mo Federated Church.

If you are not a veteran church-goer, you might not recognize the value of these tomes, or the wonderful hidden culture they represent. These little spiral-bound books are THE CHURCH. Open their pages and you'll smell the wonderful aromas of

Community Favorites II

Compiled by
Wakarusa Presbyterian Church
Wakarusa, Kansas

a church supper. You'll see a bunch of women in aprons rushing around to serve up their very best to their own and the

If you've ever served on a church fundraising committee, you will recognize the old staple Church Cookbook.

community at large. You'll hear the gossip and the expressions of concern for a sick or dying member. You'll feel the expressions of love and creativity in the beauty of the bounty implied in those pages.

But I did not fully appreciate that plastic spiral-bound treasure that stood on my cookbook stand. Not until I looked all the way through it last week. Sure, I knew it would feature recipes by many of my relatives and new friends that I've come to know since joining Wakarusa Presbyterian. I just had no idea that my cousin had written some recipes into some of the blank margins at the ends of sections.

Even more surprising was the emotion one of those hand-written recipes could invoke. Sure, I appreciated seeing her much-loved donut recipe and her prolific search for the ultimate sugar cookie and cinnamon roll. But what brought me to tears was seeing the label: Anne's Corn Chowder.

It wasn't even my corn chowder. It came from an old issue of *Midwest Living Magazine*. But that was the dish I served one cold

March day when she and her husband (now my hand-me-down husband) came to our house in Cameron, MO for a visit. I served a big pot of sausage-corn chowder seasoned with marjoram and rosemary and carbed-up with diced potatoes and a serving of blueberry muffins that day. Poor Wayne! He didn't eat any of it because, as I later learned, he is just a meat and potatoes guy who stoutly refuses to veer from the tried-and-true.

It's not the food, it's the company

Memories gushed out when I saw that recipe. Memories of all the good times, the laughs, the common interests we shared as cousins and sister-friends. And that's probably the chief benefit of cookbooks and their individual recipes. It's not about the delicious food, but the people who cook them and share them.

In addition to seeing Linda's handwritten recipes, I can open this little blue cookbook and immediately spot Helen Ramshaw's Strawberry Parfait Pie, or Beverly Nicholson's Strawberry-Pretzel Dessert (can you tell I'm hungry for homegrown berries?) I know these women, so feel I can trust these recipes to be tried and true, as well as delicious. I've seen photos on Facebook of Evelyn Davis's molasses wheat bread and my mouth waters just reading Linda Combes' recipe for banana split cake. My late Aunt Neva's cornbread dressing is in this book, as well as Aunt Delora's barbecue sauce (actually her late mother-in-law's concoction, it contains a pound of candy red hots!).

My real reason for starting this blog today was to share one of those recipes. When I gathered the courage to burn sugar to make my Aunt Gene's Best Burnt Sugar Cake in the World, I posted a photo of the resulting three-layer miracle. That led to a few Facebook friends asking for the recipe. Never one to let a good chance for a blog post go by, I'm including it here. But read the warning label.

Burning sugar is not for the faint-hearted

In the weeks approaching my Aunt Gene's 95th birthday anniversary, we always aimed to have a cooking lesson on burning sugar. But her health and constant hospice home visits conspired against us. The Friday before her birthday, I mustered enough courage to attempt the recipe that had earned her so many accolades.

This burning sugar process is one big chemistry lesson. Here's how it goes:

In a four-quart, coated Dutch Oven (enamel coated cast iron seems to work best, but don't use one of those cancer-causing silicone things) sprinkle one cup of sugar evenly over the bottom. Begin to melt the sugar slowly, over medium heat, stirring constantly. But before you even begin to burn the sugar, put a small pan of one cup water on the stove to boil.

As the sugar melts, stir faster, all the while looking for a distinctive caramel or light-brown color. The lighter the color, the lighter tasting the sugar. Light brown will give you a caramel taste, while a darker brown will provide an almost molasses flavor, which is what Aunt Gene always aimed for. But don't go too far into the dark side or you will have bitter syrup. (Does that sound like a moral lesson?) Once you reach the preferred color, put on a pair of oven mitts or gloves, pull the boiling mess off the burner, wait a little while, and pour in the cup of boiling water, taking care to stand back and not be burned by the resulting steam. Aunt Gene says to be ready with the lid to cover it immediately. Somewhere in there, plan to stir it again. Once the syrup is cooled, you will be using it for the cake batter and the icing.

An elbow-grease and butter Burnt Sugar Cake

13-1/2 T. Crisco or Butter (the thought of that much Crisco made me gag, so butter it was.)

3 egg yolks (save the whites)

2-1/2 cups sugar

Cream the above until fluffy. (This is when I love my KitchenAid stand mixer) Beat the three egg whites and fold into the mixture. (I tried to call Aunt Gene to see if that should be to stiff peak state but she was taking a nap)

Add 3 cups flour and 2 cups water and cream together until dissolved. (Next time I plan to experiment and add cake flour instead of regular flour. This is one heavy puppy of a cake.)

Mix the following ingredients in a small bowl or Pyrex measuring cup:

9 T. burnt sugar

3/4 cup Flour

1-1/2 tsp. vanilla

3 tsp. baking powder

1/4 tsp. salt

Add to the ingredients already in the mixing bowl. Note: the baking powder will possibly foam in true chemistry experiment mode, depending on what order you add everything, but just shrug your shoulders like I did and keep on keepin' on.

(And again, I tried to call Aunt Gene, because her recipe did not have salt. I think salt belongs in every recipe, so there you have it. Use your own judgment here.)

Bake that voluminous, heavy batter in three 9" cake pans lined with parchment or waxed paper and sprayed with Pam®, then floured (Sheesh! More flour?)

Frosting:

1 stick butter

6 T burnt sugar

1 box (1 lb.) powdered sugar

1 tsp. vanilla

Aunt Gene always cooked the butter and burnt sugar to a boil, then added the powdered sugar, stirred like crazy, then poured it and spread it on a cooled cake. I did the lazy woman version:

put the softened butter and other ingredients in the stand mixer bowl, covered it with a splatter shield and mixed the heck out of it, seemingly forever, stopping periodically to use a spatula to scrape the sides.

Better than winning a bake-off

The ultimate reward of gathering enough of my foolhardy wits to make the above recipe was seeing Aunt Gene's face light up as we placed that cake on her walker seat. And the frosting on the scene? Hearing her say it tasted just like hers.

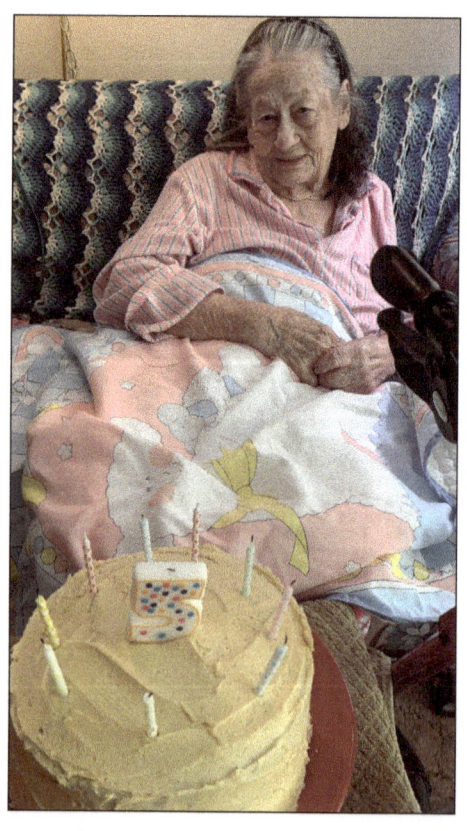

Aunt Gene's burnt sugar birthday cake, the first one she didn't have to make herself.

Journaling Through May

May 3, 2020

Wayne got head-butted yesterday by a cow. Three times. He has a nasty bruise on his upper thigh and walks with a painful limp. He may not be moving very well today.

May 7, 2020

The most exciting thing I did yesterday was consult with client Debra Lynn by Zoom about her book cover. When I shared my screen with her, we were able to collaborate to finesse the cover. She and her artist friend could see in real time what I was doing.

Jared, Wayne's granddaughter's husband, came over Sunday to help me get my two computers talking to each other so I could transfer files. In the process, we discovered my laser printer is too old, so I ordered a new one. The post office just called for me to come and pick it up. It's too big and heavy to get in the mail truck.

I know I've been operating way too long with old equipment and outdated software. But who'd have thought a 70-year-old woman would need these things? Yet I am so pumped and excited about learning all these new things. And really motivated by the discoveries in formatting and design that I'm making.

May 8

This transition from winter to spring seems endless. A cold front came through last night, bringing 3/10 inch of rain and blowing our swing over again. It's now 48 degrees with a brisk north wind. But my picture window view shows me the amazing, varied hues of green in the distant tree line. The view is framed below by our purple irises in bloom.

I have mixed feelings about the possible end of the pandemic. I like not having to rush to water aerobics class, to chorus rehearsals and to Kansas City once a week. I like not feeling fragmented and guilty. I love the feeling of accomplishment from focusing on cleaning and reorganizing. Yesterday I reorganized my office and got my new printer in operation. Baked some oatmeal blueberry muffins. I actually logged an entire day of food on Fitness Pal (except for the ice cream sandwich).

Part of me doesn't want the stay-at-home, social isolation to end. At the same time, I long to see and hug my son and grandkids. But then it struck me that I need to make more of an effort to communicate with friends and family. While I will never run out of things to do or learn, I can sure stand to re-focus my efforts on quality communications with others.

May 10—Mother's Day

Memory is such a fickle commodity. We recall things so imperfectly and through the prism of our own lifetime of experiences. Yesterday Wayne drove around Lake Shawnee for me after we went to the Farmers Market. I did get to FaceTime with my son and we had a pretty good visit while he was watching my grandson ride his bike and while he was painting his wife's Mother's Day gift. He surprised me by saying that the pandemic has really made him reorder his priorities and realize what is most important in life. I'm not sure I would have made that discovery if this had happened when I was in my late thirties like he is.

Church friends Jeanne and George Emley came over yesterday and we gave them two elderberry starts and a jar of frozen elderberry juice from last year's crop. They've raised their own fryer chickens for 30 years and never bought a chicken from the grocery store. This pandemic is really causing people to look at buying meat direct from the farm again.

May 13, 2020

Wayne and I are getting on each other's last nerves. He must be in constant pain from being injured by the cow. And probably tired of having to hook up the septic tank pump to empty the excess water from the top of the tank into the hay field in order to prevent it backing up into the house.

Our sewage system junction boxes have partially collapsed and will need to be dug up and repaired or replaced. Now that we're home most of the time, maybe the toilets are getting flushed too often and the washing machine and dishwasher are getting heavier than normal usage.

Our irises bloomed profusely in the Spring of 2020, almost as if making up for the isolation and sorrows brought on by the pandemic.

May 17, 2020

Yesterday the Kansas Authors Club, an organization of writers I joined last year, held its first meeting on Zoom. Most of the members are poets, which surprises me. We had a read-around and I shared part of my work on my Peace Corps memoir, the chapter where I talk about infant mortality. Janet, the club president, said it was riveting. I hope so. I sure need to gain more traction on it. I'm learning that writers are hungry for affirmation. I'm also learning, in the middle of the pandemic, that I'm finding inspiration everywhere. Poetry now comes to me every time I take a photo outdoors of a flower, a sunset, storm clouds...

This morning I took a photo of a little stone bunny that looked like he was resting on a purple clematis bloom and called it "Stone on Petal." If I think about it long enough, I'm sure I can come up with a prose poem. Okay, just wrote one. These things just seem to write themselves. Maybe this is why many of the author club members are poets. We're all older and maybe more in touch with our souls.

Today, while cool and gray, is so peaceful a Sunday. A hawk riding the currents blackens the sky for just a second and I watch those breezes *animate the full-fleshed leaves of our beautifully shaped oak. I bask in the onset of a promising Sabbath, full of potential, even though we're out of the habit of gathering to worship. There are other ways to celebrate now, and many other forms of prayer than communal.*

May 19, 2020

My dream this morning was about Covid 19. I dreamed I was in Walmart buying cleaning supplies and someone took my temperature. They were sending me to the hospital immediately and I was frantically trying to find my purse and retrieve the items I had already picked up. The next scene was in the hospital, where nurses were handing me tons of pills and I was dropping all of them.

Maybe the dream was prompted by going to my first in-person board meeting yesterday for the mental health agency I serve. It felt so strange driving by myself; almost like I had forgotten how to drive. The roads are still pretty deserted.

A former employee, Lisa, messaged me about a book she had proofed for a friend who was ready to take the next step with it. In the message Lisa also told me her daughter now has Covid 19 and has to go barefoot because of the horrible symptom of Covid toes.

After all of this Covid stuff, when I woke up, the first thought I had was to tell Wayne where my passwords are, then to add them to a file on my computers. I also told him he should give my business inventory to Cheri if I die of Covid, and asked him where I could find his passwords.

Some of this angst may be due to Aunt Gene turning 95 yesterday and the unusual way we celebrated the event by having a parade of cars go through her circle drive and wave at her as she sat by her picture window.

Last night's Zoom chorus rehearsal had an interesting twist when our director, Susan, assigned us to do a karaoke song, record it and send it to her. My first thought was to do Garth Brooks' "The Dance." The idea behind the assignment was to learn to love our voices. This will be good for me as I'm still learning to love myself as a person instead of merely trying to see love reflected in someone else's eyes.

Memorial Day Journaling

Memorial Day passed us by without much in the way of commemorating. A pandemic and tons of rain tend to keep us holed up inside these days, despite some gradual re-openings of things besides grocery stores.

We did put out the flag, but made no visits to cemeteries to lay fresh flowers on the graves of loved ones. I usually enjoy the family custom. It began when my Grandma Garrett loaded me in her old car with tin-foil covered coffee cans stuffed with freshly-cut peonies. Maybe that's why those smelly, loud blossoms are still my favorite flower in the world.

Aunt Delora dropped by this morning for the first time since the pandemic began. I had sent her a text message asking how she'd been, since we hadn't seen even a glimpse of her lately. We live less than a mile apart and we used to see her once a week. My inquiry into her well-being prompted her to show up a few minutes later with a sack full of treasures: photos of my mother and father and some irreplaceable family mementos.

I started a new Facebook group during the early months of Covid aimed at my cousins and capturing family memories of our grandparents.

The Storm Rages

Father, give us the humility which realizes its ignorance, admits its mistakes, recognizes its need, welcomes advice, accepts rebuke. Help us always to praise rather than criticize, to sympathize rather than discourage, to build rather than destroy, and to think of people at their best rather than at their worst.—William Barclay

Dreams of My Deceased Father and Other Rrelatives

June 2, 2020

I am learning the need to limit my blue screen time following a restless night of poor-quality sleep. In addition to the ear worm from chorus last night, the thermostat is messed up and won't cool enough. We changed sheets and they're hot, so that may have made for restless sleep. But I was in front of my computer for more than 8 hours yesterday.

On Mondays, since we do laundry anyway, I guess I should switch things up to a housecleaning day and stay off the computer except for chorus.

June 8

Got up at 5:15 after dreaming about my dad. In the dream, he had made a life for himself without us knowing. I only recognized him because of the dented, beat-up old roaster pan of my mom's that he had in his possession. I picked it up and recognized and touched every familiar dent and scratch and held it lovingly, turning it over to examine it, then washing it carefully. I think I then went with my

Facebook Post

A week of Venturing Out milestones: First in-person doctor visit, hair appointment and seeing grandkids. Capped off by an amazing sunset and then an incredible moonrise. We have so much to be grateful for in the midst of chaos.

dad as he and several relatives got in two motorcycle side cars to go for a ride. When they got back, I teased my aunts. We all had something green and phosphorescent on our hands. I took it to be frosting and licked my fingers, then wiped them off on my aunt's blouses. We all laughed. My emotions during the dream were elation, love, joy…especially at coming back full circle to my father and his family. But later I was sad because my dad had no time for me, as he had to talk to several men who needed his advice about farming. In analyzing the dream, I think the roaster pan was my life, with all its dents and scratches. I am just now recognizing all the bumps, dents and scratches I've endured, naming each trauma. And I know my father is alive, just in another dimension, as are other relatives.

In praying just now I remembered another segment of the dream. I was running. I felt so energized, and I didn't hurt. I avoided a running path for a bit and made my own path on a grassy knoll while I observed the well-traveled road below me. I knew I would get there eventually, and things would be smoother. For now, I was happy to be running.

Facebook Post

June 24, 2020– Put my sewing machine to good use this week making soft, stretchy face masks for the grandkids. Sure wish they didn't have to wear them to school this fall.

Losing Track of Time

Saturday, July 11, 2020

Strange thing this morning. I lost a day. Went to my pill box and could not figure out why Friday's compartment was empty. Had to look at my Apple watch to see what day it was. I spent July 4 home alone because Wayne was in the hay field. Surprisingly, I didn't feel sorry for myself when I realized that I'm not entitled to entertainment. The lack of expected festivities usually serves my purposes anyway. I'm always working or reading. But I am starting to see the need to look up and around sometimes and get out from under the yoke of all work and no play.

July 20

This morning I saw a Facebook ad for a typewriter keyboard; a mechanical one that connects to a tablet or phone. Has this pandemic caused us to value the things of our past more fully? I hope so. That might explain my dream this morning about the value and resurgence of books vs. electronic media.

July 24

This morning's dream was about allergies, maybe something to do with supper last night–birthday cake and ice cream for Wayne's grandson at his stepdaughter's house, followed by popcorn in front of the TV.

Spent a few hours yesterday searching for images for book client Debra Lynn's next book, trying to capture her vision of a dark knight coming out of a fire, parted by a white dahlia. We both loved what I came up with and it made me realize anew that I love the creative aspects of book cover design. I really get in the flow or the zone and lose track of time. And I just also realized that I used to crave recognition and affirmation, but now it almost makes me uncomfortable. Maybe it's because I used to do things in order to get approval. Now I do them to help others or just for the joy of being creative and using my talents.

August 6

Another profound dream. Aunt Gene was getting ready to dispose of one of two matching antique lamps that I inherited with this house. It was red porcelain with a colonial scene painted on it. I've never liked those lamps. I see them as garish. But when she started to put it away in storage, she put it with a mostly clear glass shade and suddenly I saw its beauty. Similarly, I took a good look at a folding antique rocker that belonged to my dad. In fact, it had his photo on the back of the chair. I hadn't valued it previously, because the dark finish was age-checked and flaking off. Suddenly, I realized that the chair had only one layer of varnish that could easily be removed. The chair could be restored to its original beauty. I decided to tackle the project.

*I think this dream has to do with my conversation yesterday with writing partner Cheri, about her own dream involving Personal Chapters. Suddenly, the window of my vision has been peeled away and I'm looking at an exciting scene. I can see the beauty of the road we're about to travel. All it took was for Cheri to tell me what Heavenly Father told her in **her** dream–"All my children have stories to tell."*

August 14

Our bedroom ceiling fan and light frequently pop on in the middle of the night. Wayne says we need to re-program the remote for a different frequency. When it woke me up at 5 a.m. today I knew I should get up and journal, but not before tackling my to-do list. Yet somehow my brain doesn't want to engage yet.

Am I overwhelmed with too many projects? Am I too self-critical? Yesterday I did a Facebook Live segment and all I can do now is Monday Morning Quarterback myself. I started too early. The camera angle emphasized my books too much. I looked up at my computer screen too much.

I think this is called self-sabotage. Must be time for a brain dump. Here are the things occupying real estate in my head: Terry's family history book, Debra's next book, Linda Karoub's novel, Betty Swisher's book on her brother, my Brazil memoir, my music, Kansas Authors Club, Breakthrough House (a local mental health agency), getting the city house ready to list to while trying to downsize and simplify here, visiting

Aunt Gene, not seeing my son and grandkids. I'm sure I've forgotten something else that plagues me at 5 a.m.

August 15, Feast of the Assumption of Mary and Rita's birthday.

A birthday post from Rita's (my ex-mother-in-law) family members was the first thing I saw upon opening Facebook this morning. Would love to see her again. I will never forget her words when my mother died, "I will be your mother now." And a few weeks ago when I visited Aunt Sally, (my late stepfather's sister) she said, "I'm your family."

Gratitude washes over me for the people who have pulled me through difficulties and into the blessings I enjoy now, God be praised.

As I walked out to get the paper this morning, I feasted my eyes on the rays of the sun streaming through the clouds, so I took a few photos. As I looked up the road I saw the reason Wayne had gone downstairs late last night–he smelled a skunk, which was now dead and lying on the road As I admired a black outline in the sky gracefully soaring and swooping, I realized it  *was a turkey vulture waiting to work on the skunk. It perched in the top of a tree next to my cousin's pond. I photographed that with the sun rays streaming behind it. The scene became a metaphor for the hidden evil that lurks in our lives, mostly unnoticed. But God is always there, and He sends warriors on wings to clean up the carrion.*

*At the front door I photographed two hibiscuses, side by side. It also morphed into a metaphor for the mentors and companions we've had. Capping such wonderful imagery were the words of a prayer in my daily reflections: "Do **with** me whatever you must in order to do **through** me whatever you will."*

83

August 17

Cousin Larry is having a heart ablation today. Praying for a good outcome. Then I learned that friends in Hamilton, (where I operated my newspaper for 27 years) were about to lose their home. I wonder how many others are facing this scenario right now?

Church was so meaningful yesterday. Pastor Mike Kuner's sermon was thought-provoking. He asked me before church to help him film services and upload them to YouTube. Which makes me recall the reaction of the Kansas Authors Club members when they learned I could edit video and had a YouTube Channel. That is a skill I never thought I would learn or make use of. It sure seems to be in demand these days.

August 20

"Help me to use the grace You've given me so freely and pay it forward." That concluded my prayer this morning after reading scripture about the wedding guests–the ones who didn't want to take the time from their busy schedules to attend the feast. And the ones who didn't wear the proper attire.

I know that all I'm doing these days is an attempt to pay my blessings forward. But sometimes I get in my own way. I feel so bad about my memoir session this week. I seemed so determined to share my blog with the girls in that group, so I read it. I shouldn't have. It wasn't doing them any good. I think we're all burned out from Zooming instead of actually connecting, too reliant on digital and not on old analog. It's also showing up in chorus in the number of women who are taking a leave of absence or just not showing up for Zoom rehearsal.

August 25

Last night I tried to pass the song "Let Freedom Ring" in Zoom sectional rehearsals, only to realize there were two places I'd been rehearsing wrong notes. While I was singing, my son called me, making my audio falter. Then I learned I was "scooping" (starting on the wrong pitch, then sliding up to the correct one) into the onset phrases, a problem I've had from the beginning. I almost started to cry from frustration, a feeling of ineptitude and from disappointment at not being able to talk to my son.

Blog:
Burning Hummingbird Nectar
The dangers of multi-tasking through a pandemic

I had just started getting into the focus and flow of writing when, in a panic, I remembered the pan of water I had put on to boil for hummingbird nectar.

It boiled dry, but it didn't set off a smoke alarm. We don't need one of those. We have dogs.

But this is not the first-time my multi-tasking has almost resulted in disaster. That pan got put on the stove before I mopped the floor… before I went to take a shower… before I ran downstairs to put a few more things in the laundry. And before I dried my hair and woke up this computer.

No wonder my mother always punished me for daydreaming my way through life. If I didn't have my nose in a book to avoid chores, I had my head in the clouds pretending I was a stand-in for Shirley Temple in **The Littlest Rebel,** while multi-tasking by listening to *"The Overture of 1812"* on my stereo. Sometimes I even re-read that favorite childhood book at night, under the bed sheets, with the aid of a flashlight. No wonder I needed glasses by fifth grade.

Like many of my writing friends, I'm cursed with a multi-tasking brain. I'd rather be writing or thinking about writing while I'm doing mundane chores. It's no fun doing all the things required for daily living or playing nice with others.

Yesterday, while picking grapes, my mind wanted to be occupied with grape metaphors instead of what was in front of me. Boy are there a ton of those cute little metaphors, beginning with the ones in the Bible. And whether I'm picking grapes or doing any dull chore, my head fills with future book titles, blog topics, and things to add to my Type A to-do lists.

I also considered, there in the vines, how to be better organized at picking and at life. Should I pick grapes one-by-one, leaving the green ones to ripen on the vines? Or would it be better to pick an entire cluster and discard the green ones as I wash and sort them? Now there's a metaphor worth developing...perhaps while stirring the grape jelly.

Do all multi-taskers also have the habit of talking to themselves and inanimate objects? Or is that just an older woman like me?

I began to talk to the grapes.

"Why don't you guys ripen at the same time?"

"How in the world have you survived not being attacked by the racoons and birds this year?"

"Is my late cousin Linda guarding you at night from the coon foodfests? Does she want to make sure I get jelly made for her mom and brother Larry?"

"Why aren't you bigger, plumper? Do I need to prune you all better in March?"

"Why don't I just let the rest of you ripen a little more. Who cares if the birds or the coons find you before I get back for a second picking?"

Sounds nutty, doesn't it? I talk to the green beans too. And the tomato cutworms. Now here's the warning label: We know advancing age can show us how multi-tasking and forgetfulness can lead to danger.

My husband doesn't know (and please, don't tell him) that I talk to the grapes and build mental metaphors to help me zoom through the drudgery of things I have to do so I can hurry and get to the things I want to do. Just like I did when I was a kid.

I'm not so old that I can't recognize my own faults. I know that if I had ever been allowed to write as much as I wanted or endlessly metaphorize (is that even a word?) my way through life I'd no doubt have morphed into a mystic or a hermit. Or just a total nutcase.

The pandemic of 2020 has accelerated creative output for me and many of my friends. We've finally been able to get to some of the fun tasks we've been putting on the back burner. I just hope my fellow multi-taskers do not let their pans boil dry.

Why won't grapes all ripen at the same time? It would make it so much easier for multi-taskers who would prefer to be writing instead of picking grapes.

Swept Overboard

Very often, "what happened" takes years to reveal itself. It takes courage to confront our actions, peel back the layers of trauma in our lives, and expose the raw truth of our past. But this is where healing begins.—Oprah Winfrey

September Sweeps In Bringing Loss, Struggles, New Purpose

September 5, 2020

Yesterday was grueling. I signed listing papers on the house in the city. But had to do a lot of cleaning there first. Wayne got up on the roof and re-attached a chimney cap, cut brush, got rid of all of daughter Kelly's fabric planters and tried to charge

Drive-by birthday parties became the new way to celebrate during the first days of the pandemic. Our grandson turned six on September 1.

some of the power tools in the shed. We got there at 9:15 and didn't leave until 3:15. A long, hard day and my knee was in agony on the way home. We have to go back before Wednesday to get the house ready for photos. The listing will go live Thursday.

September 6

The day was consumed with technology challenges; namely, trying to film church services correctly and get the video uploaded to YouTube. It took all day. I had filmed the Facebook Live with my iPhone on landscape, so it showed up sideways in the feed.

September 7-Labor Day

Went to the city to work on the house. I shampooed carpet on the back porch while Wayne cut brush. Washed windows and blinds and did several other things I can't remember now. Wayne came home and got on the mower to use the harrow on the dirt my

Facebook Post, Sept. 12, 2020–My house in the city went on the market this week. Sad to say goodbye but life marches on. Former brother-in-law Robert (Chad) Chadwick is the listing agent. He was our buyers agent back in 2011 when Marshall and I bought it.

cousin Terry's ex, Rusty, (he's a heavy equipment operator) brought in as fill after he repaired all the sewer lateral junction boxes. What a Labor Day! We did nothing but labor.

September 11

I think I've been tried by a jury of one (myself) and found guilty. In I Corinthians 9, Paul writes, "...I drive my body and train it for fear that, after having preached to others, I myself should be disqualified."

September 15

Our chorus's first in-person rehearsal was last night. Being able to see each other and sing together, even through a mask, was like a slice of heaven.

September 19

I have got to stop responding to Facebook ads that promise to teach me how to set up *Facebook Live* videos that will sell whatever I have to sell, or templates that will help me set up e-books quickly, along with social media posts. My time is being hacked, even by an online "un-hackable" group I follow. I'm like a butterfly that flits everywhere at once, landing for nectar but seeing a better source somewhere else, then flying away to a better spot before I've even gathered any nectar. In the process my wings are getting tired. They're drooping sadly and in need of an energy boost. I give away my pollen to others in need, because I think that's what I'm supposed to do. I do little to help or satisfy my own needs. Once again, I'm not even thinking I deserve to do something for myself.

At today's *Kansas Authors Club* zoom I was asked to consider taking on the president's position.

September 21

Fall is definitely here. I am getting concerned about my recent bouts with impatience and irritation. It could be due to the medicine I'm taking. Spent yesterday catching up on some of the social media learning groups I've bought into and sort of re-imagining our business. I'm realizing the need to really focus on the needs of clients instead of our need to sell product. I'm finding right now that connection is what we most crave in these days of Covid. Fulfillment also comes to mind.

September 25

In the middle of formatting Terry's book yesterday, I came to a sudden realization. What I'm doing now with book publishing is so much like newspaper publishing. I'm a jack of all trades, doing a broad spectrum of things, some creative, some boring and routine. And, just like when I was in the newspaper business, when all I wanted was to write, instead, I had to make sure I could pay the employees, so I had to always look for advertising income. At least now I don't have to try to sell advertising in a tight market.

Saturday, September 26

Woke up with the hymn "He Touched Me" in my head. Just now I had such a sense of gratitude at the privilege of being alive and being here in Kansas, back where I started out. I really have a wonderful life, despite its rocky early years. And sometimes I ask myself why I continue to work so hard instead of just relaxing and enjoying retirement. Then I realize it's such a multi-faceted thing. I do this because...

1. I can. *Thanks to God, my health is good and getting better.*

2. I'm a late bloomer. *I didn't start my real career until I "retired," didn't start a family until I was 34, didn't realize God's plan for me until age 60.*

3. I have God-given talents that I feel compelled to use *and a mission assigned by God. My only concern in all of this is how I might be neglecting Wayne. He is such a helpmate, companion and friend. He's not jealous of me or my activities. I think he worries that I take on too much. (I do.) And I love how he also sacrifices to serve others, the way he went to the house of a chorus friend in my place and got her brother out of his wheelchair and onto his garden tractor.*

Yesterday so many insights and inspirations came to me. Too bad most of them were more things to do.

Getting Crazy Busy

October 6

I reluctantly committed to serve as district president of Kansas Authors Club.

October 9

Yesterday was the first public performance of our chorus after the Christmas show last year. I was surprised at myself and how much I enjoyed sharing our gift of harmony. I made eye contact with individuals in the audience and lost self-consciousness as we sang the words of pride in country with feeling. It was a wonderful experience and I sure want more of it.

Yesterday I got out Linda's old bread machine and made some whole wheat bread. That was satisfying too.

October 10

Last night Wayne and I went to his Army Guard friend's retirement party. Talk about a band of brothers! I was amazed at how all these men seemed to respect and revere Wayne. One of them, Matt, even called him Dad. As we went around the table and introduced ourselves, when it came to Wayne, he surprised me by becoming emotional. Those guys mean so much to him. He literally gave them all wings, coaching them into maturity as experienced pilots.

October 13

I'm worried about myself. I had it in my head that our second anniversary was today. Yet it was yesterday. I didn't even get to town to get an anniversary card for Wayne. He had two for me. So, I hurried up and spent the morning composing a poem for him. It was good, and he was pleased. But I'm still worried about my head. Where is it? What am I thinking about when I should be listening? Last year I gave Wayne a watercolor painting by author client and artist Lila Bartel of him with our dog Brandy. This year he got a poem. But I did bake a cake and frost it. And we did go out to lunch at Longhorn, so we marked the occasion. I've just got to start getting better sleep and stop juggling so many balls.

October 15

Dreams and emotions. It's been a slow letting go. Yesterday we ran to the city to take a new TV to Rosie. Her roommate died, probably of Covid, and the TV in their room belonged to her. While in the city we went to the house and brought up the last boxes of business inventory. Every item fit inside the three cabinets in the garage here. I'm so pleased with that. But then I dreamed of Marshall, and of a sad, slow good-bye. Maybe it was his spirit working through my dreams as he lets go himself. In the dream I was reluctant, as I knew I would face difficulties. I knew I would miss his laughter and the good times we shared. But I finally knew he would be okay. As I placed an order Sunday night for a Facebook memory book, my sadness over my marriage to Marshall and over leaving the house we shared resurfaced. It was there again yesterday in the continued disassembling of the house. Such an ache in the pit of my stomach. I so loved that house and took so much pride in it. On another recent time we were there I tried to pray in the sunroom, where I had always prayed, but I could not recapture the soul and sense of that space. I guess that's another sign of the need to say good-bye and let go emotionally of who and what I was and who and what we were in that house.

Blog

Ten Ways to Give New Structure to Your Days

You would think that having all our routines disrupted since March would enable us to seize the day. We have more hours now that we're not taking trips or socializing with friends over lunch. One would assume we would also be able to instill healthier habits and more structure in our lives.

At least some of us are writing our memoirs or autobiographies, taking photos and nature walks. We're composing poetry, taking time to sit at the piano or bringing out the dusty guitar. During this pandemic, we should at least try to enjoy life a little more, once we get our chores out of the way.

We used to mark time with wall calendars and analog wrist watches. Maybe the fact that our lives are all on digital demand explains why some of us lose track of time.

Last weekend I looked at the calendar and expressed shock and outrage that we were almost out of October. Where was my time going? It was October 1 just yesterday!

I somehow frittered away the hours and the days of the month. I binge-watched a Netflix series. Instead of cleaning the house, I told myself that required too much effort. Besides, no one came to visit (the only reason for cleaning, right?)

I didn't wear makeup. Why bother? I don't see anyone anymore. I only go to the grocery store once every two weeks, and then I'm incognito with a mask over my face. I stay in my pajamas until 11 a.m. some days. And sometimes I skip taking a shower. (Sorry. Too much information?)

Please tell me I am not the only one with newly-discovered lethargy these days. And now that it's getting darker earlier, the potential for slipping into depression is huge.

Not sure if I would know what day it was without my handy

medications dispenser. The important thing is remembering to fill it.

How do you structure your days and weeks now that we're all forced to be homebodies? I used to define and structure my weeks with Mondays being laundry and cleaning days, Wednesdays being a travel day when I drove to Kansas City to spend time with my grandkids and then visit the nursing home to see my former stepmother-in-law. The routines at both those places included reading and playing with the grandkids and playing a few hands of gin rummy with Rosie. But the nursing home is still on lockdown and due to multiple concerns about family members with health issues, my son is still on virtual quarantine and our communications 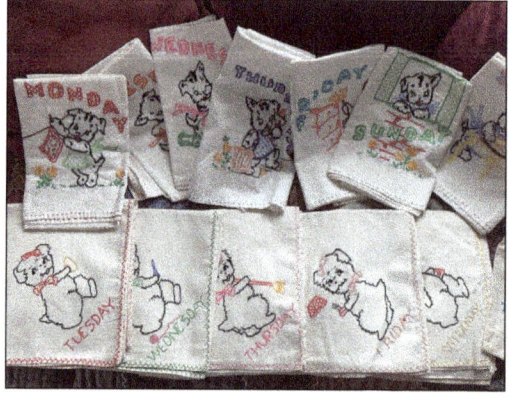 limited to FaceTime and Zoom. Like so many other American workers, his company's physical space has been closed, possibly for good, as everyone shifts to working from home.

As a writer and retired newspaper publisher, I made the work-at-home shift six years ago. But making much headway with housework or writing has suffered greatly since March. I need a system and a structure like my own mother and her mother both had. Their days and months always passed quickly with the help of structured routines and chores. Remember the tea-towels embroidered with the days of the week and the names of tasks they had to accomplish each day?

Dish drying towels used to help us keep track of our days and our chores. Now the only time we use these things may be during holiday meals, when all those extra dishes won't fit in the dishwasher. Then someone washes while someone else dries. Usually there is a carpe diem moment and conversation actually occurs.

Confession: I missed out on a full dose of my mother or my grandmother's DNA and work ethic. Today, into the vacuum of time I used to devote to visiting family, comes a combination of Murphy's Law and the Peter Principle. I tend to rise to my own level of incompetence, wherein anything that can go wrong usually does. The day gets filled up somehow but sadly lacks any visible results.

A few days ago, when I began to feel overwhelmed with all my undone chores and responsibilities, I recalled and began doing something I once tasked my newspaper employees with: I started keeping a time log. I wanted to figure out exactly what was happening to my hours and my days. At the same time, I came up with a list that I think can provide a better structure for my days.

I'm going to share it with you in case you are in the "spinning wheels" mode too.

Ten ways to structure your pandemic schedule
1. Clean or reorganize something
Even if it's just a countertop or the wastebasket. Did any of you have a mother or grandmother who spouted little proverbs like "Cleanliness is next to Godliness?" Cleaning just one thing will make you feel less guilt.

This morning when I got out of the shower (no, that did not make it on this list) I took the time to spray a shower cleaner on the walls and shower fixtures. That led to seeing the need for cleaning the bathroom countertop. It took all of five minutes–time enough for my hair to drip dry. Efficient, yes?

2. Bake or cook or make something
After emptying the dishwasher today, I hauled out my cousin's old bread machine and started baking a loaf of honey whole wheat

bread. In a few hours it will fill the house with wonderful smells. Yesterday I cut apart those packaged cookies you buy in the dairy case at the store and baked those. Later I made sloppy Joes in one pot and chili in a second pot by dividing three packages of ground beef. Now I have leftovers and two extra meals.

3. Learn something

In these Google, Covid, Zoom-filled days, as businesses scramble to reach customers in the virtual sphere, we have no excuse for not learning new things every day. And any new bit of trivia counts as learning.

This past week, after watching a report on the Kansas City Chiefs, I wanted to learn a little more about the players who formed the 1970 Super Bowl team coached by Hank Stram. A Google search uncovered a name from my youth–Jan Stenerud. My eyes opened wide in surprise to learn this gifted Norwegian kicker was not a U. S. citizen when he played for the home team. Even more surprising? He was an active duty member of the Army National Guard while he played football.

In addition to sports trivia, I find myself clicking the "Join" button on free seminars and workshops dealing with the craft of writing. There is no excuse these days for failing to pursue our quest for new knowledge to improve or enrich our lives. It's all out there with just the click of a mouse or the tip of your finger pressing on a link.

4. Read something

Imagine my smug satisfaction at putting that task on the list! My favorite activity since childhood was to step away from reality and go on mental adventures in the pages of a book. When I ran out of kid lit, I ransacked my mother's bookshelves, even reading a thick historic novel on Benedict Arnold at age 11 and actually enjoyed it.

However, to the above simple admonition to read, I need to add:

finish what you start and only read one book at a time. (Although that will never happen for me.)

5. Write something
If you are not a lifelong writer like me, not to worry. A grocery list counts. An email works. A love letter to your honey will do really well. And if you don't write something every day? Count yourself as one of many who are helping cursive writing die a slow, painful death. How's that for inducing guilt?

6. Do an act of service for someone or something
If we have assumed a late-life role as a caregiver...if we live with someone...if we have elderly relatives...if we do volunteer work for an organization or belong to a church...we have multiple opportunities to do an act of service. I am lucky to have a husband who serves as a wonderful role model of service. He goes about his selfless acts quietly, without need for recognition. But then, he began doing that while growing up on a farm. He continued it with a 32-year career in the military.

7. Pray for someone or something
When I start to feel sorry for myself and my disrupted routines, I look around and know others who really have a reason to be sad or depressed. They may have lost a loved one this year. They may have lost a job or a home. Their mental illness may have worsened. If I know them, or know about them, they make it on my prayer list. Today I returned to an old habit of writing down my prayer petitions. I know how powerful the practice of writing is to make our wishes manifest. And we all know how much our world needs prayers for healing during this pandemic.

8. Find a reason to laugh or cry about something
Sometimes, when we numb out in depression or lethargy, we need reminders that we are still part of the world, that this requires

our participation. Nothing does better as a reminder than to find a reason to laugh. Or to just let it all out with a good cry. Both are soul cleansers. My husband reads the joke section of *Reader's Digest.* I laugh at my own jokes. Then I cry because I'm such a slow learner.

9. Exercise something

This was a total afterthought, added only because I knew it should be. I hate exercise. If you hate exercise too, find things to do that count for exercise without realizing it's a workout. I like the theory that even short bursts of activity count. Thus, going up and down the stairs in my house will get me a 71-year-old's "good enough" badge, as will walking to the road to pick up the mail or the daily newspaper. One of these days, when I'm feeling extra ambitious and energetic, I'll look for the link to the chair yoga class I purchased a month ago and only accessed once. Most days I will probably give myself a pass by exercising my brain (see numbers 3,4 and 5 above.)

10. Enjoy someone or something

Visit an elderly relative and listen to his or her sage advice. Call a friend you haven't talked to in a long while. Look through your high school yearbook. Go through all those greeting cards you've collected over the decades. Pick up the needlework you used to enjoy and finish that creative project. Color in an adult coloring book. Get on Pinterest and dream about the things you could do if you only had the time and the money. But then stop cold when you realize you do have the time now. And now that my list is appearing in this blog, I'll be able to check off the "write something" for today.

Facebook Live

When Halloween Candy Highlights a War Between Body and Brain

This morning's Bible reading from Romans fit my current frame of mind. My body is at war with my mind. All. The. Time.

Licensed Adobe Stock photo #282956236 By Steve Cukrov

I'm trying to eat healthy. My mind is full of good intentions for healthy eating, but my body went out and bought several bags of Halloween candy for all the trick or treaters. The ones we never have. And then my body, which isn't connected to my brain, put those bags of candy really close to the couch where I finally collapse at night to watch TV with my husband.

And then we have the disconnect between my mind wanting to accomplish so much in a day and my body that has not yet learned to say no. I think in my brain I can still do as much as I did when I was 30. Consequently, only about half of my to-do list gets crossed off. Then I start feeling guilty and thinking there's no way to get all these things done unless I stay up for 24 hours straight. The stress kicks in, I eat more Halloween candy and I start to feel resentful and look for someone to blame or project my guilt onto. And ta-da! I blame it on my parents and the work ethic they only halfway instilled in my DNA. And I blame my grandparents. They were so driven to rise above poverty–at least my grandfather was– that he used his kids as slave labor on the farm. He took them out of school in the eighth grade.

In turn, my parents were driven to succeed and prove themselves. I got some of that compulsion from them.

Here I am, supposed to be retired, and I'm so busy with volunteer obligations and client obligations that I don't feel like I can take care of myself or relax or spend quality time with loved ones.

I justify all of this by telling my brain that it's my Christian duty to serve God and others first and myself last. But my body doesn't get the message and rebels. My brain and my DNA thinks that God is telling me to do even more. I get in an endless cycle of compulsive behavior and guilt. When it gets overwhelming, I give up, finally, and turn it over to God. I tell him, "Here, You handle this because I can't anymore."

Then I remember the scripture that says, "I can do all things through Christ, who strengthens me."

That's when I relax and start journaling again and I suddenly have a fresh perspective. That's when I also realize that every project I complete...every deadline I meet...has always been God working in and through me. It hasn't been my own will or my own talents, or even the work ethic I may have inherited from my parents and grandparents.

And if I wasn't so forgetful and hurried and stressed, I wouldn't have to learn that lesson over and over. I need to put a sticky note on my forehead that says, "Here I am, Lord. I come to do Your will, not mine." Then I'd have to remember to take it off my forehead and read it or look in a mirror. Maybe I'd better just paste it on the bathroom mirror to begin with.

How about you? Do you have a strong work ethic that gets in the way of being in the moment and going with the flow? You might want to journal about that and explore how your attitudes about work and being a faithful servant of God have been formed. Maybe you'll discover, like I did, that it's good to remember to let go and let God.

Technology Word Cloud, created by author in freewordcloudgenerator.com.

Blog

Keeping Up With Digital Technology: Do We Need to Reset Our Defaults?

Just when we got a little more comfortable in our living rooms, they rearranged the furniture.

The metaphor here refers to digital technology...you know, the stuff we've become addicted to and rely on now to keep us from total isolation. And ignorance. But digital technology is also capable of driving us stark raving mad.

That's what happened to me last Sunday. If I hadn't been in church, I would have erupted and said some really bad words.

We were about to start the weekly livestream of our church service. Each Sunday I've been able to set my iPad on a tripod, mount an external microphone on the top, aim it all at the pastor and hit a start button on the church's Facebook Live group. It's a good feeling to see familiar names pop on to watch the live church service. Yeah, they get to stay in their PJs and drink their coffee while hearing the weekly sermon, while we had to get semi-dressed up. But it makes me feel like a good Girl Scout to enable this virtual service.

But last Sunday, the feed did not happen. Or it happened in fits and starts as I saw a message on screen that said I was out of data.

What? I had just increased the plan to unlimited so I wouldn't run out of data. I fumed through the entire service, missed the point of the sermon and then resorted to holding my iPhone on my knee to film the last of the service.

Just wait until I get home, I said under my breath to nameless national phone company. Yeah, well, good luck with that, they probably answered. It's called customer service. But no longer does it involve a customer actually getting to connect with a live agent. Nowadays we have chat services for that. More people working from home in their jammies and drinking their coffee and getting paid for it.

Oh, you can try to get a live agent from customer service on a Sunday, but will be told the wait could be longer, as call volume is higher than normal. (Isn't it always?).

"Would you like to hold your place in line and let us call you back at this number?" the dialogue box asks.

"Yes, please." Fifteen minutes pass. The phone rings. A mechanical robot voice intones, "Your customer service representative will be with you shortly."

Fifteen more minutes pass. No customer service representative. By now I've been to the bathroom, started making lunch and cleaned the stove. I hang up in disgust.

Fifteen minutes more–text message from unnamed phone company appears on my screen.

"May I help you?"

One hour and 27 minutes later, after wearing out my fingers typing messages to a robot (or was this a real person sitting in Timbuktu drinking coffee in their pajamas?) I learn that the extra data I ordered online two weeks ago does not go into effect until November 19. Would you like it to go into effect today?

Duh! Would I be typing and mis-typing with my fat fingers on a tiny phone screen just because it's fun? Now, $189 and a giant headache later, I think we have a plan that will allow me to stream our church services each week without worrying about running out of data.

Except that the church board voted two days later to suspend in-person services until the Covid-19 infection rates in the county go down considerably.

Since that fateful Sunday, I've compiled at least three more examples of how this harsh new technology era is about to turn many of us into screaming meanies.

• People who want to open a pdf file on a PC laptop running Windows 10 now frequently encounter problems with Microsoft's new browser, Edge. That new browser will soon replace Internet Explorer. There are work arounds to the new difficulties. They require resetting your defaults in the browser.

• This week one of my book clients tried to send me photos from her new iPhone. The photos came to me in some kind of unrecognizable format. It wasn't a *jpeg*. I couldn't place it in my client's book. She had to go reset a bunch of defaults, educate herself about this new extension on her photos (done to save storage space) and get them back to me so I could format Chapter 13 of her book. (Is there a bit of superstition at work here?)

• Thinking I knew what I was doing, I recently paid $149 to get a premium plan through Zoom so I could interview guests in Zoom and broadcast simultaneously to Facebook Live. Except that it does not work because of something called latency. My internet service provider only gives us 1 megabyte per second on upload speeds and 3 point something on download. That's all we can get out here in rural Kansas. I order the latest technology from our local ISP. But when the technician arrives, he lets us know that the nearest tower for the most modern equipment is 30 miles away—too far to pick up a signal. We are stuck in Lodi again. Why did the saleswoman not realize that? Grrrr!

Trying Not to be a Covid Crybaby Once Again

I'm trying so hard to be positive, to be a good girl and not a Covid crybaby. In fact, I see all the silver linings we've all snatched from the pandemic clouds surrounding us. I've been grateful for the ability to strengthen and maintain friendships on virtual platforms these many months of adjusting to new realities. When I encounter difficulties, I know I need to follow my husband's advice and take three deep breaths.

As a Covid Thanksgiving gift to readers, I want to share some humble advice to help others navigate this painful new reality we face with technology. Here are a few things I've learned when I've stepped outside of the frustration zone and into the lifelong learning zone

• Keep an open, agile mind and a lifelong learner perspective. The pandemic has made so many businesses and educational institutions move to virtual platforms. And while the learning curve can be frustrating, there are awesome opportunities here to keep our minds agile and adaptable. If you want to learn a new skill or understand how to do something, search for a YouTube video or an online tutorial or even an entire class.

• Try to be patient, even if you want to throw the *&^% computer or phone through a window and bite your husband's head off. As the unintended object of my frustrations always urges me…take three deep breaths. Maybe even sleep on the problem. Get away from it. Take a walk outside and get your head out of electronics for a bit. You'll come back to the situation with a new, refreshed attitude and the realization that if the world ended tomorrow, if you succumbed to Covid, this little frustration or learning curve would not matter a bit.

• Ask for help. Alternatively, be content with having things that don't operate at warp speed or with total efficiency. I often ask my son for help. He knows so much more than I do about digital technology. And while we tried not to be those aggravating older

Americans who can't get their TV to operate correctly, we've had to own our disabilities. A year or more ago, we asked my son's help to set up a way for our old analog surround sound system and DVD player to talk to our Smart TV. He hasn't had the time. And now he doesn't travel, thanks to Covid. So we just never watch DVDs and I use my hearing aids to listen to movies. Thank God I learned how to stream Netflix and Prime. And now, thanks to my new data plan with my phone company, I can finally watch *Yellowstone* on Hulu. For six months anyway, while the free plan continues.

•Don't multi-task when you are learning or trying to understand a new technology wrinkle. Don't take your laptop or phone to the bathroom and expect to complete two jobs at once.

• If it's not broken, try to avoid fixing or buying new. Operate on old platforms and equipment until you *have* to get new stuff. I have two older desktop computers. One of them is way beyond support and the other is nearing its obsolescence. But thanks to new subscription services, rather than installed software, I can continue using the computer by connecting to online platforms. The minute you buy a new computer or piece of equipment, a new learning curve begins. Avoid it if you can. Upgrade only if you must.

•Be grateful for small victories and inches of progress. This week I read half of **The Velveteen Rabbit** to my grandkids on FaceTime. They appeared to listen and watch as I turned the camera around and aimed it at the colorful pages. Since I can't be with them right now, that was enough.

And boy howdy, was I ever excited when we told Alexa to print our shopping list! She complied and managed to find the nearest printer on the network without any help from us.

•Be aware that the more you learn about technology, the more you may be called upon to use your new knowledge to help others.

But isn't that what we are on earth for? To lift up each other?

• Be aware of your limitations. While you may get tasked with helping your church, your neighbor, or your favorite organization with your tech skills, be aware of your limitations and be open to continued learning. There are a lot of things I know enough about to be dangerous. I tried to help out my local Sweet Adelines group with a virtual chorus project. While I learned a lot about editing audio tracks and putting them together on one track in Garage Band, I didn't have the foundational knowledge of unit vocal sound and how to manipulate audio to produce a satisfying project. That should have been left to a professional with experience.

• Be ready to make choices. My husband's favorite saying is "We have one decision to make in life—participate or not participate." My ancillary to his saying is "Once you make the decision, be prepared to pay the price."

The price we pay for trying to stay on top of technology? Dry eyes from staring at screens too long. Thinner hair from pulling out strands in frustration. Lost moments and quality time with loved ones while we're engrossed in our electronics trying to figure out the latest upgrade.

It's all a matter of balance. May the digital and analog God be with us all.

Pandemic-Driven Misunderstandings

October 24, 2020

Went to the city to drop off my granddaughter's birthday present and attend Wayne's great-granddaughter's birthday party. My son and I had an awful texting misunderstanding. It was 36 degrees, and he wanted us to stay outside to give my granddaughter her present. I lost it. We both texted things that we later regretted. I even brought up my late second husband in trying to understand why we couldn't see the grandkids indoors. Was I still paying for mistakes I had made with my son by exposing him to Marshall's dysfunction and narcissism? (Turns out that had nothing whatsoever to do with the situation. But I would only learn that much later.)

We dropped the present off on the front porch and left without seeing any of them.

When we got to the great-granddaughter's birthday party, it was packed. No one was wearing a mask. We were shocked and uncomfortable. We had no idea there would be that many people there.

October 31

Cheri has been here since Wednesday and goes home today. We've had a type of strategic planning retreat built around a writer's retreat put on by Flourish Writers, an online Christian group. Watching some of the sessions together has given us direction and motivation. Through our brainstorming we've gained knowledge and a new task list. We've also become more committed to our purpose and our mission. We've keyed in on our individual strengths and adopted a divide-and-conquer plan. We know we don't have time to waste. I'm grappling with age and mortality and she is preparing for another lockdown and the coming of the savior. She is detail-oriented while I am deadline driven. Yesterday we filmed a Facebook Live at Auburn Cemetery that emphasized connections to our families and our Christian beliefs. We started each work session and each meal with prayer, thus connecting us and renewing our dedication to doing God's work.

November 6

Yesterday was exhausting mentally. Cheri and I are putting a lot of pressure on ourselves, but we're sure it's necessary. We did a test of Zoom to Facebook Live and there were issues.

November 7

Sent a conciliatory email to my son but haven't heard back.

I just finished shampooing carpets where the dogs have had accidents. All the windows are open and a warm, brisk breeze is blowing through the house—the final airing out before a cold front comes through tonight.

This morning I recorded my Christmas karaoke song for chorus and edited it in Garage Band. Another new thing I've learned to do.

November 9

Up since 4:15 a.m. in a blur of pain from the arthritis flareup in my knee. Started asking myself what things I can still do while my legs are incapacitated. I need to ask Cheri to pray for me. I really need to talk to my son but I don't think he has the bandwidth for me. Just like I didn't have the bandwidth for my mother, even when she was in her last months of life.

Karma. Just as Marshall predicted.

Anne Spry

The Storm is Calmed, at Least for Now

Creativity is the first vaccine against Covid.*–Anonymous*

Facebook Live:
Learning the Benefits of Online Collaborations

When the pandemic began, everyone I know began moving previously social and business communications online. Like many of my clients and friends, we signed up for a Zoom account and pretended this was the most natural thing in the world. It was not, but we adjusted.

My first Zoom interaction occurred with a client on a book cover. She had an artist friend who was looking over her shoulder and making suggestions. I made the revisions live and got their immediate feedback.

Next, I began collaborating via Zoom with another client, Theresa Stahl, who had an ambitious and beautifully illustrated family history book to publish. Thanks to Zoom, we could collaborate in real time as I used my design software to manipulate pictures and type according to her suggestions.

This new way of interacting with others even filtered into volunteer organizations I belonged to that had to hold meetings in a new way. Our Sweet Adelines group had to start singing on Zoom, with our mics muted, so we wouldn't lose momentum in learning new songs. The mental health organization I served as a board member had to conduct meetings via zoom.

In looking back at those early Zoom days, I. have to admit there were many positive things that came out of it. Those new ways allowed many of us to work from home, save gas and time. But I think it also ushered in an exciting trend for all types of collaboration.

Just this week I collaborated with a singing friend to revise a script for our Christmas show—a script we basically wrote together on Zoom.

The best example of collaboration I've been involved in lately has been with my business partner and friend Cheri. We're doing videos together tomorrow. We've written books together and have several more planned.

Are there any ways you can collaborate with your distant family members? The pandemic gave me a strong motivation to work on an extended family history. I started a new family group dedicated to that effort, and we've already shared some wonderful old family movies and photographs on the site. I think it's drawn us closer to each other as a family.

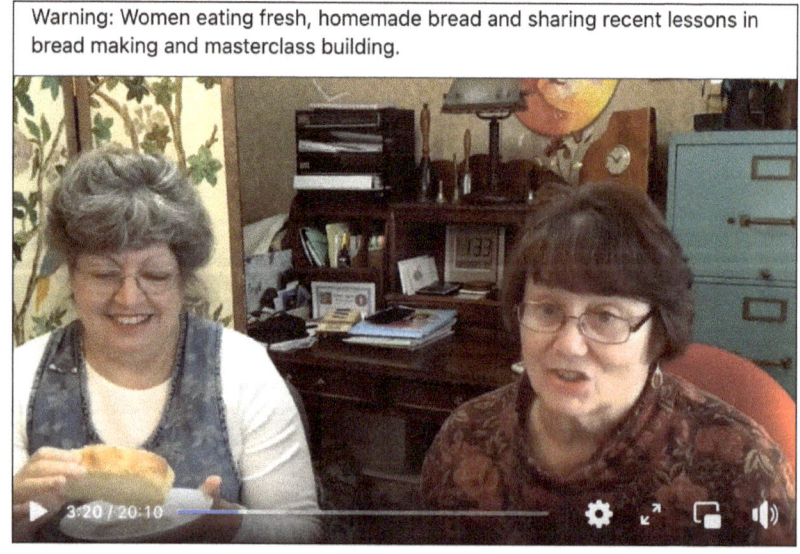

Warning: Women eating fresh, homemade bread and sharing recent lessons in bread making and masterclass building.

https://tinyurl.com/BakingBreadandSharingLessons

Business partner Cheri (left) and I learned many new ways of collaborating during the pandemic. But we had the privilege of doing some in-person collaborating like this Facebook Live session on the joys of bread baking.

Covid Thanksgiving Facebook Posts

November 26, 2020

Happy Turkey Day to all. May you cope with the non-traditional environment of isolation and emerge after the celebrating infection-free, full of hope and grateful for any tender mercies encountered during this holiday season.

November 27, 2020

It was just the two of us yesterday.
So strange, so quiet. I took a picture of him,
he took one of me. No noise but our chewing.
Neither of us had seconds.
We needed to mark the odd occasion,
record it for posterity, noting the austerity.
No lively conversation, so real celebration.
But later we rejoiced in phone calls and texts
and a grandson's quick visit to drop off
some ham loaves made in honor of a
deceased family member. It recalled connections
and cemented a bond, reminding us
of the purpose and meaning of this day.
Let us pray for the return of exuberance next year,
even of chaos and over-indulgence. And may we all
be thankful for this gentle pause in the year
that most of us chose caution and isolation
so that the next one can be a traditional celebration.

Journaling Through a Strange New Holiday Season

Monday, November 30, 2020

My CPAP monitor says I had 7.5 hours of therapy. I feel fairly well rested, even though I got up twice with our dog Ro-Ro and woke up several more times. Wayne and I are so stressed over this dog since her rear-end skin surgery right before Thanksgiving. We met my cousin Theresa Tucker, our veterinarian, at her office yesterday at noon. She sedated Rose, washed her rear and pulled off the blood clots, glued her skin back together where it had pulled loose from the adhesive stitches, gave her morphine and penicillin and sent us home with special food; food she now won't eat.

I think Dr. Theresa is secretly worried the operation will fail. I'm worried that we'll kill the poor dog. We're supposed to put antibiotic ointment on her butt, but she fights it so much it may be better to not do it. She won't eat this morning. I worry she won't trust us to feed her food that doesn't contain medicine.

Maybe my obsessive worry is driving Wayne batty. He snaps and barks. We went to sleep without kissing each other good night. That's only happened a few times since we got married.

Heavenly Father, all the angels and saints, help us! Our holiday has been ruined and we don't yet see better days because we are so stressed and concerned for this dog. Maybe we should have spent the rest of her life wiping her butt instead of having the surgery.

Dec. 2

Our dog Ro-Ro is now incarcerated at Dr. Tucker's clinic.

Saturday, December 5

Up at 5 a.m. to go to the bathroom. Freddy the cat came up meowing. No way to get back to sleep. I think I'm supposed to journal. At least that's what brought me down here, thinking I'd get in touch with myself through writing and have a few moments of illumination.

And now I'm distracted with all the cat hair on my t-shirt after picking the cat up to comfort him. I'm also praying that Ro-Ro is okay and that she comes home to enjoy a few more years of life with us, even if it means insulin shots twice a day.

As I got up this morning another thing struck me: The theme of my life has been trying to find a home. Then I realized that my home has always been inside my heart, no matter where the physical home of the day was. Home is where my spirit resides, where God lives.

All my life I've tried to control the physical aspects of my home, the way the furniture is arranged, how peaceful, serene and welcoming it is. Only now have I realized that my destiny is to be a pilgrim. Yet I've resisted that; fought against it. Even now, living in Wayne and Linda's former house, I try to control the environment with my own personal touches, my own Feng Shui. Yet I long to clean out, simplify and make this a well-organized, clutter-free home. But I don't live in a vacuum. I'm here with a man who is sentimental about physical items and still grappling with the death of his former wife.

Nothing is permanent; we take nothing, not even our clay house bodies with us when we die. We only take the essence of our souls, our love, our desire to be of service to others, our good hearts. And we can never lose that. The tragedy is that some of us never find the homes of our hearts and souls. We wander around blindly, longing desperately for what we feel is lacking in us and allowing ourselves to be swayed or led along unfulfilling paths, dead-end roads.

Like many who've gone before me, I've sought a home in religious doctrine and in physical church buildings with religious and spiritual leaders and inside self-development books and courses. I've sought homes with husbands, preferring companionship over solitude, giving away my selfhood and autonomy in exchange for shelter and security and material things. I've taken the issues and insecurities of others and made them my own and told myself I'm not worthy of anything but dysfunction and chaos.

All along, the home I've been seeking has been staring at me in the mirror. I must still have miles to walk to find a place of tranquility and peace. Every day that I come closer to knowing and loving myself is a step closer to heaven and the home I've always had. I will go to my true home someday, but only after I've led myself and maybe others down the path I finally see His light illuminating.

For now, I need to stop obsessing and trying to control the way the path looks to me and to others. That's not my job. Doing so will only distract me from walking home. There are many paths home and many rooms in that heavenly mansion. No room is better than others, none holier or brighter or more loved by God. No reason for jealousy or strife in those rooms. The food at the banquet will taste the same, no matter which room we're in. It will be seasoned with universal love and free of any influence of the great adversary.

There, in those many rooms, we will tell the stories of how we finally found our way home. We will tell of our amazing adventures along the road and speak of the wonders of the paths that finally converged...paths that encapsulated and illuminated what we were sent out to learn and discover as perpetual pilgrims.

Monday, December 7

Pearl Harbor Day, Medicare Enrollment Day, the Day Anne Finally Got Her Sh*** Together and Got in the Holiday Spirit...maybe.

Yesterday I managed to complete livestreaming the church service without too many glitches. But we have to dispense with YouTube music. Got a message that the recording would be muted, at least the portion with the music copyright violation.

From a Kary Oberbrunner Facebook Live: An image chalked on tiles: "One day you will tell your story of how you've overcome what you're going through now, and it will become part of someone else's survival guide."

Tuesday, December 8

We don't have to take Ro-Ro to the vet every morning and evening now to try to treat the diabetes she has developed post-surgery. We think her insulin is regulated at 5 units. But we still may have to call for an appetite stimulant.

Got quite a bit done yesterday. A little more decorating. Made peanut clusters that need to be thrown away because I used raw Spanish peanuts. Big mistake. The big thing I got done was finally figuring out what was going on with the files in Terry Stahl's book.

Anne Spry

Facebook Live

Finding Life's Purpose
After a Lot of Mistakes

While reading scripture this week about Mary saying yes to God and the angel Gabriel, the accompanying reflection caused me to think about my own yes to God's calling on my life. I'm proud to say that yes, I have. I've found meaning and purpose in my life. But it sure was a long time coming. And I sure did make a lot of mistakes and bad choices along the way.

This second week of Advent has been a good time to do a lot of soul searching. I had lunch with a new publisher friend, who is about 15 years my junior. She was almost upset with herself when she discovered my age. She said, "There's no way you are that old." And then she said, "Why is it that all of the women I admire and hang out with these days are older than 70? Why do all of you look younger than you are? And what am I supposed to learn from you all?"

My immediate internal response was that she's supposed to learn it's never too late to discover a purpose and a passion. But like my friend, the first requirement is that you have to be walking on a spiritual path. She has been a seeker for several years and I'm sure she has already found the right path, the right purpose.

And that's our secret sauce. Finding our life purpose and learning the lessons we're destined for from the moment of birth is so transformative. When you find what you were sent here to do, somehow your steps get quicker, your energy skyrockets and the blessings begin flowing in. That's not to say you won't have sad days or bad days or drop back into negative, judgmental habits. It's not to say that this process of finding yourself happens overnight

125

or that it doesn't come with a high cost.

But I believe we're each gifted with certain skills and then given an assignment to complete in this classroom of life on earth. It takes some of us, like me, a long time to get on a spiritual path, to come into harmony with ourselves and our purpose. I discovered that the first step in getting on the right path to complete my assignment was to forgive myself for taking so long to wake up and find the path. I first had to stop thinking I was the center of the universe or in control of anything. I had to learn to pray first and relinquish control of most of the details of life and the actions of everybody around me. I had to say, "Here I am, God. Do with me what you will." Just like Mary, I had to learn to trust and obey. When I did, that's when the magic began happening and the puzzle pieces started falling into place without my having to see the border first.

How about you? What is your story of finding your purpose? I'll bet it's a beautiful one. And if you are not sure if you've found your calling in life, it may be time to sit and meditate about that and then start journaling about it, by hand. You might be really surprised at the things your writing hand will reveal to you when you start putting pen to paper.

In fact, your story of finding purpose in your life is probably the most important one you can leave for your family. Write to reveal for yourself and your family the costs and the benefits of figuring out what you were designed for. If you haven't already bought all your Christmas presents, writing your story of finding purpose would be the most meaningful thing you can give to your family this year.

Making Treats to Induce the Spirit of a Covid Christmas

Sunday, December 13, 2020

I finally redeemed myself somewhat in the holiday department yesterday. Made a tasty batch of peanut clusters with regular Spanish peanuts, not raw ones, but then ate too many myself. Addressed Christmas cards to church members, finished decorating the tree and presided over an author club meeting.

I am really looking forward to church this morning since Nyla Suffron, our music director, will be playing the piano. Today I hope to get other cards addressed, a Christmas letter written, fudge or cookies and an apple salad made, and quality time spent with Wayne.

Monday, December 14

Yesterday I got the church livestream done, (managed to sing with Nyla), addressed cards, used the Instant Pot to cook a pork roast and finally made an apple salad. Also watched the Kansas City Chiefs football game. I'm not sure I accomplished anything else but struggling to play a few hands of Free Cell Solitaire on my iPad. What a time waste!

December 15

*Thanks to widespread Covid infections, I have pretty much stayed at home and ordered presents from catalogs. Yesterday I finally got my annual holiday letter composed. But I had to re-word it after Wayne read it. And I feel so bad. It needed re-wording. It was full of pride and arrogance. That's what today's scripture reading is about. Perhaps the pandemic and its social isolation has made me more selfish and self-centered. I think I need an attitude adjustment and a new self-mantra...a Thumper-ism...**If you can't say something nice, don't say nothin' at all.***

Saturday, December 19

Wayne and I went out for Christmas shopping yesterday, mainly for grandkids. Started at Walmart and I was amazed at how often I had to stop at vivid, colorful displays of gift items, especially *Pioneer Woman* stuff.

Picked up the toys on our list, then headed to Sam's Club. Came out with fewer items than we've ever picked up there. By then I was hungry and hurting, but we went to Barnes and Noble anyway. The store setup since the pandemic hit was totally disconcerting. It looks bare in there. Had to take a nap when we got home. Then didn't do much except work on a video Christmas card project for the grandkids.

Facebook Post

December 27, 2020–Another incredible, God-textured dawn in rural Kansas and elsewhere. A reminder that those we have lost this year to Covid are in a place of perpetually beautiful sunrises. I received word this morning that my former brother-in-law, John Tezon, died from Covid in the VA Hospital in Columbia, MO. May he rest in the beautiful dawns of eternity.

Journaling into a New Year

Wednesday, Dec. 30, 2020

Twelve more days in the Christmas season. More time to pave the way for a better new year, a fresh start at offering my gifts and myself to God, to start anew at seeking His kingdom. Despite all the tragedies of 2020, I find myself filled with hope and joyful expectations.

Thursday, January 7

What an eventful month already! My identity has been stolen and I have a sales contract on the house. The country is in turmoil from Trump supporters taking over the capitol building in D.C. as Congress was attempting to certify electoral college votes. Four of them were shot, at least one fatally, and the nation is outraged. What struck me in watching the live coverage last night is that the protestors look like us: white, middle-class, late fifties to sixties.

I know this feels like a desecration because it happened in the building where our laws are made, the building that symbolizes democracy. It feels similar to the attacks on 9/11 of our financial center.

I did a "Memoir Mentors Facebook Live" that offered the following list of questions and suggested my followers write down their answers as part of their personal history or memoir:

Democracy and the Principles We Hold Dear

1. Where and how did you learn about our government and our own responsibilities for maintaining a democracy? Was it in a civics class? Were you forced to pass a test on your state's constitution and the U. S. Constitution? Do you recall anything from those classes?

2. Where were you when President John F. Kennedy was shot? What was your reaction? How about your parents' reactions?

3. Where were you and what was your reaction on 9/11 when we were basically attacked by foreign elements on U.S. soil for the first time? How did that make you feel? Describe your reactions as you watched the planes hit the twin towers and then saw the towers collapse? How did your attitudes about our country change at that time?

4. Describe how you felt last week as you watched the assault on the U. S. Capital. What do you predict will be the ultimate result of that attack? And do you think that the potential loss of constitutional freedoms in the wake of the attack will be justifiable?

5. Do you always vote in local, state and national elections? How do you determine who to vote for?

6. Where do you turn for information on candidates and issues on election ballots? What media do you rely on these days for your news and information?

7. Have you ever run for a local office such as school board, township board, county office or higher? If so, describe the experience, the outcome and what you learned from it.

8. Have you ever actively participated in promoting a campaign for an issue or a candidate you believed in? What did that look like and what did you learn?

9. As you have grown older and wiser, how have your attitudes changed about politics and government? Have you felt a loss of interest and/or influence and individual power?

10. What information and advice would you leave for your children and grandchildren about their duties as a citizen to help uphold democratic ideals?

11. How would you express and explain your attitudes on the following national issues?
- Capital punishment
- Immigration
- Welfare programs
- Subsidy programs such as farm programs
- Conspiracy theories
- Far right and far left organizations
- Gun control
- Freedom of religion and separation of church and state
- Freedom of speech
- Abortion

Friday, January 8, 2021

Cheri and I spent three hours on Zoom yesterday. We started with prayer, which I gave, and we began outlining content for our memoir book. It is taking a totally new direction. Instead of offering a product focus, it promotes the value and benefits of memoir as a tool for connection, self-discovery, healing, and uncovering of our souls – all through our stories and storytelling. We want to have this published by November, unless God wants us to accelerate things.

Woke up at 5 a.m. feeling rested. Immediately found the notebook detailing our estimated proceeds from the sale of the house and am feeling prompted to refigure things based on the offer in our contract, all with an eye to considering whether to buy an RV. I want to look at this for business and personal travel, and as a place for company to stay, maybe even as a mobile safe haven in the event of total national chaos.

Saturday, January 9

Today is my late brother Rick's birthday. So much life gone, for all of us. My dream this morning featured me traveling a well-used main road and veering off of it and into a pasture. There I came across three archaeologists from a government agency. I finally recognized them as people I had previously interviewed for a feature article. I told them I'd been in the business for 50 years but was finally retiring. I was sad and not sure what my next step was. During my interactions, I realized I didn't have my mask on and retrieved three from the car. They were all dirty; debris clogged their filters, but I had to use one.

Yesterday I pushed myself to get my to-do list done. Had a marketing meeting for chorus. Worked on my script for Memoir Mentors. Recorded the Facebook Live then uploaded revisions to **Divine Mirror,** the book for client Debra Lynn. Started to do another computer task and all of a sudden, I was done. I realized how much I've been pushing myself, how mentally tired I am. I came down to spend time with Wayne. Took a nap. Took some Christmas things to the basement. Wayne took the rest. As we deliver the last of our Christmas gifts and two birthday gifts in the city today, the holidays will officially be over. Then I hope I can get that fresh start I advocated in my Facebook Live.

Sunday, January 10

We went on a whirlwind trip to the city yesterday. It was enjoyable in the places we were able to stay for a bit. Even being with our grandkids outside and in the garage, despite how cold it was, was enjoyable.

January 11

At 3:30 I woke up from a profound dream. Should have journaled it then but will have to try now. Something about soldiers making a long, arduous trip literally tied up in a ball, squished into a box, unable to move. They arrived at their graves, were unfolded and laid to rest. I stood over them and promised to not let their stories die. I would be sure the world knew how they suffered and what they achieved.

Yesterday I took some ham soup, cinnamon rolls, and a cherry strudel to Aunt Gene and visited briefly with her. She was worried about her son (my cousin) Larry. She is stubbornly resisting being catheterized by Hospice staff. Can't say I blame her.

Notes through January 15

Was able to weed through Christmas decorations in the basement and take overflow to God's Storehouse, a local thrift store that accepts donations. Did a workshop for the author club on planning your writing year.

Rosie tested positive for Covid on 1/15/21. She was moved to isolation at the nursing home.

I started knee injections again. The last round began Sept. 5, 2018.

January 19

We have a contract for the sale of my house in the city.

I'm working with Cheri on story arcs. The narrative arc of my story includes a traumatic childhood that led to me hiding from others and myself, feeling as if everyone was watching me and ready to judge and criticize. It was only through writing that I received affirmation. I could not express feelings and emotions outwardly. But I could on paper. I over-compensated by being responsible, taking on more than a child should, then escaped in books. I got in trouble for reading and really got in trouble at age 13 for calling a boy on the phone. I spent my childhood trying to please and appease a critical, judgmental mother who had her own self-esteem issues.

Topic for Facebook Live: We are not our mistakes. A lifelong battle to not define ourselves by what we do. What is our identity? If it's our job, our profession, what happens to that when we retire?

January 22

At 3:30 I woke up feeling the urgent need to write, to continue with my mother's story. Maybe she was dictating.

These are the words that came to mind: I hated my mother as an adolescent. I scorned her as a child because of her immaturity and selfishness. As a teen, I pretended a friend's mother was my own, even shunning the company of my biological mom. As a young adult, I abandoned Mother physically and emotionally. Until the day I needed her to tell me why her example as a strong, proud, independent woman had not worked for me. I learned it hadn't ever worked for her either. Our divorces brought us together in pain and long-delayed empathy. From our great healing, love dawned. It spawned forgiveness and charity for fate and for each other. In maturity we shared our talents. She learned to play the organ and served her church just as I served mine. She joined a writing group and began offering a column for my newspaper. Yet my husband, whose mother was no longer alive, had to remind me constantly, "Have you called your mother?" Until the day she diagnosed her own cancer.

Finally, as a mature adult, I cherished my mother in her last days. We laughed and joked about death. We looked at photo albums and I played her organ as she selected her funeral songs. At her service I gave my mother's eulogy, nearly pushing the minister off the dais, so anxious was I to tell her story, recite her poetry, and take pride in her talent.

Now, as a motherless child approaching the same age as she was at passing, I revere my biology, my origins. I must share the story of how I traveled from hate to loving reverence and respect, from hollow emptiness to fulfillment with my new forever muse.

I look over these words–poetic and lyrical phrases that seemed to write themselves–and realize I cannot take credit for any inherent power they may contain. This saga of hatred and scorn that morphed into gentle memories to cherish was written in heaven, before either of us was born. Our mother-daughter, hate-to-love story unfolded exactly as God intended.

Tuesday, Jan. 26

Yesterday I found it so satisfying, even energizing, to arrange the office for better productivity and aesthetics. Wayne brought up the oriental screen from the city house. I think it makes a better Zoom background. It's reversible, so the back side may be better for some uses. My current files are closer now and in a stacking holder instead of spread out on a table (which is now folded and stored in a corner).

Last night at our regular chorus Zoom rehearsal with a guest speaker, I cried at the end of Sandi Wright's presentation. I didn't know the song she played, "How We Sang," (See How We Sang Today-Four Part by Sing with Jenn on YouTube) but it made me feel such an ache and longing to sing together again and in person. Suddenly, all the losses, all the trials and sacrifices of the pandemic hit me full force. It felt good to cry and release the emotions, thanks to the music. The lyrics, "I'm glad we laughed, I'm glad we cried, I'm glad we sang, oh how we sang," was the tipping-point for tears.

Blog

Handling Grief and Funerals During a Ppandemic

We said goodbye to my cousin Larry this week. Covid-19 did not do him in, but it sure did a number on his funeral plans.

Those of us who knew and loved him watched the family drama unfold. I vowed to record the story for posterity, and to maybe help others who have to bury a loved one during a pandemic. After all, we have had a paradigm shift with regard to how we are now forced to handle the business of death and dying. So many families can no longer gather at a bedside to say a final good-bye. Funeral homes have been closed. Church buildings are empty. Funeral crowds are often limited to immediate families, then tagged by the media or health department reports as super-spreaders of illness.

Where do we go with our grief in these Covid days?

Initially we worried that pandemic restrictions would leave us incapable of closure through traditional grieving rituals. Those restrictions did put a few wrinkles in the funeral, but we worked around and through them. We are Kansans, after all.

My 95-year-old aunt pushed Covid boundaries

Larry's daughters gathered around his surviving mother and included her wishes in every aspect of the planning. At 95, my Aunt Gene is still a force to be reckoned with. Admittedly, burying her two biological children has stripped her of much of her starch. But we watched in awe as her sharp mind maneuvered around Covid restrictions. If challenged or reminded she should not be planning that or doing this, she just smiled politely and pretended she couldn't hear.

Aunt Gene knew she was not supposed to have people come

to the house after the funeral or for any kind of meal. That didn't keep her from inviting everyone she talked to, from cousins to the funeral directors.

She wasn't the only one. When the hospice workers who come to the house several times a week insisted there be no visitors and absolutely no food brought in, everyone meekly acquiesced. But behind the scenes, the local church ladies put on masks and gloves and

Her granddaughter, Leslie, reads online condolences to my Aunt Gene

gathered in one of their homes to make bologna salad sandwiches from Aunt Gene's own recipe. They called my husband to come and pick them up and secretly deliver them to her house, so that any "stray illegals" who popped in before or after the funeral would be fed.

My aunt has not been out of the house for nearly two years since going on hospice care. This week her granddaughters arranged for a transport van with a lift and a wheelchair to get their grandmother to the graveside service. Then, just a few days before the service, Aunt Gene said she really wanted to see her son's body so she could have closure. Maybe she needed to make sure he was really, really dead, as that song in the Wizard of Oz goes. But we all suspect it was more a matter of pushing through those doggone Covid parameters to exert some control over a difficult situation.

The funeral home directors quickly arranged for an 11 a.m. viewing at the mortuary, followed by the 2 p.m. graveside service. That required two separate appointments with the wheelchair transport van. It also required a virtual retinue of family members to help Grandma Gene get dressed in something more attractive than flannel pajamas, then shove men's slippers over hospital socks then over edema-swollen feet, and wheel her across temporary ramps and into the van. She got a bit annoyed when someone shoved a plastic face shield over her newly-permed hair. And she flat out refused to wear a second mask underneath the shield, saying she couldn't breathe.

The Grandma retinue toted around a large bag full of hand sanitizer, water bottles, tissues and other necessities. But she was irritated to discover no one brought her glasses. And she was really disgusted to find that she had to wait at the funeral home until the van returned for the next appointment. To help her pass the time, we asked a staff member to print out the condolences, and stories of Larry that had been submitted via the online guest registry.

Online condolences can be captured, preserved

Those memories of my cousin contained veins of gold. They showed us all a side of Larry that I hadn't previously seen. They took the place of the tradition our little rural church has of allowing everyone to tell their stories orally during a funeral service. Covid has closed the building to all gatherings. But the stories got told anyway, thankfully, due to new online networks maintained by the funeral home.

At the graveside service, we were all warned to social distance. We wore masks. And scores of us showed up for what was advertised as a private family service. The older generation in our rural area–folks who watched Larry grow up, play high school football and join the Navy–they were at the cemetery, masked and safely distanced. Some of them could barely walk over the uneven cemetery ground. Someone came with a walker. When one of my relatives tired of standing, she sat down on the closest tombstone, checking first to see if the person buried there had been someone she knew. We seemed to be united in participating in an outdoor social event that was permissible during a pandemic. Luckily it was one of those rare, warm winter days.

We need familiar rituals and to hear the stories

No matter the generation, we all hungrily soaked up the pomp of the military service–from the flag-draped casket to the loud rifle reports and playing of Taps and through the flag folding and presentation by members of the Air Guard to Aunt Gene. Our spirits gained comfort from the familiarity of the ritual. Even though we had all heard the 23rd Psalm repeated by pastors at every funeral service in memory, we needed to hear it again and be soothed. But what we all really needed to hear? Stories of Larry, as told by his tearful daughter. We laughed and cried with her to hear the memories he made for his three daughters. She managed to capture some of his witty sayings. The most memorable, "Stop acting like farts in a skillet" (settle down). My favorite was her story of gathering at Larry's sister's house for family dinners, crowding into the dining room like sardines in a can, then finding it impossible to leave the table except by crawling under it.

The only thing missing was a display of photos, and a slideshow, and music

Our celebration of Cousin Larry's life contained almost all of the elements of any pre-pandemic funeral. But it did lack the display of photos depicting the highlights of his life. It lacked the slideshow playing in a perpetual loop on a screen or television monitor in front of the church. It lacked music playing in the background and it lacked congregational singing of old, familiar hymns. We had to be content with a taped version of "Taps" and a country gospel CD player version of "I Come To The Garden Alone." Those attempts at honoring funeral traditions were a welcome balm to most of us. But we wanted to do more. And so we have.

The celebration of Larry's life and the traditions and legacy of family continues now through a Facebook family group set up a few weeks ago when I stumbled across the rough beginnings of a family history book. My cousin Linda (Larry's sister) started on a family history dedicated to our grandparents way back in the 1980s. It contained photos of Grandma Junia and Grandpa Noble, photos of cousins, photos of aunts and uncles, and treasured recipes from each of them.

The cousins are now collaborating on the preservation of the stories. Cousin Mike posted a rare but grainy 16 mm scene of the family gathered around a dinner table, then another one of Grandma walking (most of us remember her always seated in a wheelchair), and yet another of some ICBM missiles being delivered to silos in Kansas. Through the comments and discussions prompted by those videos I learned that my Uncle Max helped excavate the missile silos in the area, running his bulldozer expertly in circles and down into the ground, until a crane was brought in to lift the dozer into the ever deepening hole and then out again when it was complete. Thanks to Cousin Kevin, one of many pilots in the family (a tradition that began with his dad), I also learned the difference between Atlas and Minuteman missiles. Who knew? Who cared, except us, now that we are older and want all the details. We want our history to be deeper than our reactions to a pandemic.

Meanwhile, back at a somewhat 'illegal' funeral
In addition to telling family history stories in a new Facebook group, we told more tales after Larry's funeral, while gathered "illegally" at Aunt Gene's. We ate dishes that those mysterious and unnamed hands prepared, taking off our masks just long

A 1950s 16 mm movie, filmed by my late Uncle Rex and shared by Cousin Mike on our new Facebook group, caused some of us to shed tears of gratitude and recollection.

enough to inhale the comforting flavors of cheesy potatoes, baked beans, lasagna, chocolate chip cookies, bologna salad sandwiches, and gallons of hot coffee. We excused our indulgence by labeling ourselves as immediate family. We tried to stay six feet apart, but we've all been around each other and in and out of the house so often and for several months now. Some of us have even had Covid and stayed away for several weeks. But we always come back to the nucleus, to the traditional gathering spot and one of the only homes that now archives our memories. We always gather at Aunt Gene's.

We told and preserved a few new stories in her house this week as we coped with loss and worked around pandemic restrictions. We became stronger, more resilient, more loving and better people, maybe even because we could not do exactly what we are used to doing in the grieving department.

Here's the image that remains in my head and heart from this week: My aunt leans forward from her wheelchair, peers over the top of the open casket at her handsome, gone-too-soon son dressed in blue jeans and a soft flannel shirt. and says softly, "Bye, son. I'll see you in Heaven. I'll see you soon."

The rest of us now have the job of making sure we collect all of Grandma Gene's stories and memories…before "soon" rolls around and catches us unprepared.

Riding Rainbows Through the Storms

Blog
The Death of a Community Newspaper Hits Home Hard

A Facebook post on the last day of 2020 hit me hard.

Still in pandemic holiday mode, my husband and I were sitting together on the loveseat getting ready to escape into another mind-numbing Netflix series. A scant 15 minutes prior to casting the show to our family room

Woman reading newspaper on wooden background by sebra, Adobe Stock #201472297. Licensed image used with permission

television, I had shared news of the demise of a weekly newspaper in the town I called home while attending high school. One of my classmate's comments in the group almost made me bawl. "It has run its course," she concluded, but she did mark the sadness of the death of a community newspaper.

The demise of refrigerator journalism

Her comment and my husband's reaction to my distress shocked me into an awareness of the profound global implications of this one little bit of news. It reflects and even summarizes, on a micro-level, the dramatic changes we've all endured in 2020 and in the years before that.

I had caught the beginnings of the trend even before I sold my own weekly newspaper. That's when I learned that refrigerator journalism–the trend of newspaper subscribers in the U.S. to cut out articles featuring their kids and secure them to the fridge with a

Business people reading newspaper by Rawpixel.com. Adobe Stock 193907642.
Licensed issue used with permission.

magnet–was dying. Back then, I scrambled to start a Facebook page for my newspaper so we could at least attempt to communicate with the younger generation.

Dirtying hands with soy ink

Kids back in the early 2000s did not want to get their hands dirty with soy ink. They already had their noses buried in their phones instead, and that's where they turned for news. They didn't seem to care that doing so caused a disconnect with their community, their hometowns, and any generation older than theirs.

Those changes in how we communicate and share news with each other accelerated at warp speed last year. The shuttering of one more print newspaper caused me to sputter in frustration, "Who do they (the unnamed community members and advertisers who had failed to support the newspaper enough to afford a living for the owners) think will run photos and stories of their kids on the football field or walking across the stage to get their diplomas? Or, how about births and deaths? Or an editorial that explains a local bond issue? Or photos of people running for local office?"

My husband looked at me with a wicked grin. "You know the answer to that."

"I do not!"

He repeated his statement, adding more irony and increasing his cajoling. His attitude reminded me of teachers who would put you on the spot and even embarrass you in front of the whole class to elicit an answer that was obvious to everyone but you.

Where will we get news that's terse, accurate, fair?

When I continued to insist that I did not know where people today—in the community of the defunct newspaper or elsewhere—would turn for balanced, terse, accurate, fair and unbiased local news, he glanced at my hands.

"You're holding it. You're using it."

Phones? Facebook?

"For the love of God, how will we ever educate ourselves on Facebook? How will we ever get the truth? The real story? Or the story behind the story?"

My husband's reply to my exasperation was a quiet, "It doesn't matter. They don't care. They don't feel like they need the truth. They think it doesn't affect them. Besides, most of us want to live in a bubble and make our own reality. Isn't that what we've had to do this year?"

I thought about that for a few quiet moments, then tried to look at the other side of the story myself, the way I'd been trained to do in journalism school. Then I admitted I would

Mobile news application in smartphone by terovesalainen Adobe Stock #232438285. Licensed and used with permission.

What would we have done during 2020 if we could not turn to our mobile devices to keep us connected to each other and the world?

145

have become certifiably insane from March through December of 2020 if not for Facebook and the Internet. That is where I now go for family photos and news, then share them with a husband whose military clearance level prohibits him from even having a social media account.

Thank God for Facebook, Amazon and Zoom

Thanks to social media and the Internet, I've watched multiple video workshops, joined virtual groups, attended Christmas parties via Zoom, purchased most of my Christmas presents online and shared slices of my own life. Like most of you, I've been able to keep in touch with high school classmates, longtime and new friends, and promote my own business efforts thanks to these virtual platforms.

But 2020 has shown me that, while adopting and adapting to these new forms of communication and commerce, I remain stuck in Baby Boomer ways. I like walking out to pick up my daily newspaper. I treasure the routine of snapping it open, folding it wrong side out to a feature story, while drinking a cup of tea or even eating my lunch. Try that with a smartphone and see how dirty the screen gets!

I turn to those ink-soaked newspaper pages to learn all the details of a local story; details usually absent from the brief sound bites on local television stations. I still look to print media that I can touch and books I can reverently turn the pages in to connect my head to my heart to my memory.

Who will be our community cheerleaders?

I still mourn the death of any newspaper. Every town needs a cheerleader, a watchdog, a champion and a community builder. That's what local newspapers represent. And if the print versions are all going to die, I pray to God that the online versions live. I pray that the pandemic doesn't sign the death warrants for too many more of them. Because we will miss them when they're gone. We just don't know it yet.

How will we clip articles for future reference?

If the local print newspaper were to die, I would no longer be able to clip articles about local authors to contact for programs of our Kansas Authors Club. And I would probably have missed a column by "The History Guy" this past week if it was only online. It told the delightful story of a wealthy, faithful newspaper subscriber years ago. The man loved reading the ***Topeka Capital Journal*** so much he paid in advance to have it delivered to his grave at a local cemetery. He even paid to have lights strung across his tombstone so he would have light 24/7 to read the newspaper.

Those newspaper deliveries continued until the day they were seen as less of a quaint practice and more as a crime of littering.

Are print newspaper readers just tree killers now?

And this, my friends, may be the real cause of the death of print newspapers...too many of us now see them as representing the death of too many trees.

Newspaper and Coffee by stockfotocz Adobe Stock 78826156. Licensed and used with permission.

Newspapers and cups of coffee or tea were made to go together...at least for a Baby Boomer's comforting routine.

Yellow suitcase and signpost with travel destination.Maksym Yemelyanov Adobe Stock 284708270. Licensed and used with permission.

Oh the places we'll go...or the places we used to go...or the places we'd love to go. The pandemic has shattered many travel plans.

Would You Give Up Sex If It Meant You Could Travel Again?

Thirty-eight percent of Americans would give up sex for a year just to travel again. And 80 percent of us feel that travel is part of a well-rounded life.

Wait a minute! Did I hear that right? Yesterday's headline made me stop in my tracks. Who would give up sex to travel? What program is that?

Turns out it is not a program or a new virtual reality show. Just a silly survey a travel company conducted.

149

Most of us (except my husband) have been missing traveling the past year. Traveling to see grandkids, traveling to have lunch with girlfriends or to water aerobics classes. Traveling to our getaway vacations.

My husband doesn't miss traveling because he spent 32 years as a military pilot going to places all over the world. He likes home. He'd rather be at home. Well, he's had ample time to be at home this year and he has a really good excuse not to indulge my need to travel, because we've been stuck at home in a pandemic.

And even though I traveled all over Central and South America many years ago, and even though I'm pretty content to stay home and stay busy, I miss traveling…a lot.

Vaccinations could open things up soon

I get my first Covid vaccination next Tuesday. Within a month, when I get that second shot, I'll feel free for the first time in a year. As long as I have a mask with me, I won't hesitate to get in my car and just go. But I know that it won't be the same as it was before the pandemic.

In fact, a few weeks ago I had to travel to Kansas City to sign closing documents on the sale of my house there. We had an hour to kill that day and tried to find someplace to grab a sandwich. The part of the city where we

Rustic Open Sign, Adobe Stock 92113293. By Mr Doomits, Licensed and used with permission.

Signs at local bars and restaurants may soon turn from Closed to Open.

had the closing used to be thriving. It was deserted. We're talking ghost-town, science fiction, end-of-the-world deserted! I had not imagined there would be so many businesses still shuttered.

Thus, even when we get our vaccines, even when people start traveling again, things are not going to be as easy as they were before the pandemic.

Apparently we're going to have to hold on a bit longer. We may have to even adjust our travel habits a bit once we can get back on the road. I guess travel agencies and airlines and cruise lines are recognizing that, because my cousin Susie has already received notice that trips she had planned for this year are being rescheduled for 2022.

Talk about agony!

Road Map with Navigation Icons, Adobe Stock #303097555 by Andrey Popov. Licensed and used with permission.

Have you noticed how many little red thingamabobs there are on Google Maps in your area? Follow those thingamabobs on a local journey of discovery.

What to do while we're waiting to travel again

So, what do we do while we're waiting to pursue our passions for travel and the need we have to go places? Well, I'm no expert, but I'm trying to be patient and do as many things virtually as possible. Here are some ideas that popped into my aging brain while pondering yesterday's headline:

•The first thing I plan to do is update my passport. That's been on my to-do list ever since I got remarried and changed my name.

But I keep putting it off. I want to go back to Brazil one of these days. I'd really love to go to Europe. And that brings me to the next suggestion.

• Start a bucket list of places you'd like to go. You probably already have one, or you have things already checked off a bucket travel list. But this is a fun activity. It's fun to dream and imagine the places you'll go.

• Since everything is online these days, start taking virtual trips on YouTube, or read a travel book or magazine to help grow your bucket list.

• Attend a virtual concert. I did.

• Start making a list of places you'd like to go in the state where you live. There are so many places I have yet to explore in Topeka and in Kansas. Western Kansas, with its unique limestone formations, is now at the top of my Visit Kansas bucket list.

• To help make up your places to visit list, subscribe to email lists or blogs about travel. Connect with your local tourism department and download the state travel brochure.

• Haul out your old travel photos and put them in an album, virtual or physical, and relive the places you've already been and the trips you've already taken.

• Dig out your last travel journal. If you didn't journal about your last trip, or document it in a photo book or album, start a new travel journal and write about the places you'd like to go. Also, why not just journal about your feelings and frustrations about not traveling?

• Try to recapture the memories of the most amazing trip you ever took. What did it do for your five senses? What did it sound like? Feel like? Taste and smell like? Write about that as if you're sitting down and having a face-to-face visit with your grandchildren.

If you follow any of my suggestions, I'll bet that before you know it, you'll actually be taking a trip. And for sure, you won't be taking traveling for granted. In fact, there are many things in addition to travel we won't be taking for granted anymore.

Journaling through a Miserable February

February 1, 2021

After a miserable night with my hiatal hernia plaguing me with spasms and sharp pains, I woke up determined to make better choices. No raw onions, no dairy at night, no chocolate at night, beef no more than twice a week, no more coffee in the morning, better meal planning, more vegetables and fruits, track my intake, get on the treadmill. If I can do these things consistently, I will increase my stamina, my longevity, lose more weight and lower my A1 C and avoid full-blown diabetes. Plus, I will sleep better. This has to be a line in the sand. No more miserable nights!

February 2, 2021

Another miserable night. Got up at 1:30 to take two Tylenol Arthritis pills and get an ice pack. I watched myself as if watching a stranger endure a perpetual Groundhog Day, pushing through my knee pain, trying to ignore it. I observed myself erupting in rage or just garden variety anger because my body wouldn't let me do what I wanted it to do. I could even laugh at myself from this new vantage point as I watched me trying to get our neighbor Beverly's recipe for lemon cake out of the pan, saw it totally fall apart, saw the Bundt pan break the cake plate, watched myself cuss and scream in a rage as I threw the cake and the plate in the trash. Then, from this new dispassionate place, I asked myself what I am to learn from this. My conclusion—stop trying to meet old and unnecessary expectations. Stop pushing myself so much. Try being gentle and compassionate with myself.

All of this was confirmed today as I started to plan my month and found there weren't enough slots for "work." In one moment of realization, my unbalanced life was there for me to see. But I excused it by saying that the work I do is for God, not for my own affirmation or ego gratification. I think that makes it okay. And who said life must be perfectly balanced and compartmentalized anyway? Oh, the lies we tell ourselves!

I do recognize the need to be kinder to myself, with fewer self-expectations.

Thursday, February 4

I'm watching the snow swirl around in dizzying whirlwinds. What a contrast to the warm sunshine and almost balmy breezes of yesterday! The first thing I saw on Facebook this morning was a post of an old home movie. Cousin Mike Garrett shared it on the cousins group I created. Have to remember to thank him for it and save it. Then I need to post a snippet of the video I took at Larry's funeral.

When the wind picked up at about 5 a.m., that knee started aching and throbbing. I hobble up and down stairs, one at a time. I see my neck wrinkles every time I do a Facebook Live and I cringe at how my hair color doesn't blend well with the wrinkles, yet wonder why my mental and emotional capacity seem not to age.

Saturday, February 6

It's 23 degrees and an east wind is blowing, sure to bring the snow in the forecast. Wayne will be taking Cousin Donnie to the airport in the middle of the storm's track. I think I dreamed of Donnie last night, even though the dream featured my son. In the dream I was having a house interior painted. In one room I was having a wall painted a beautiful bronze or gold to contrast with an equally rich butternut color. I marveled at the beautiful hues in each of the rooms as I walked through them—rich forest green with accents of ivory, rose pink and deep peony red. There were a few rooms left yet to decorate, but I was so content.

I woke up thinking of Cousin Donnie and the arc of his life. Rejected by his alcoholic mother and put in an orphanage, rescued by his dad and brought back to Kansas to become part of a family that had its own dysfunctions and never feeling like he fit in. Donnie was traumatized by a hellion of an elementary teacher who beat him because he couldn't read.

All our lives are so troubled, so dysfunctional. This week has been so full of family and has been truly transformational with regard to family history. I re-read my Aunt Beverly's high school autobiography and shared photos of my Hoffmeister great-great grandparents with a friend from Germany. I wrote a blog that touched the hearts of many, and my family Facebook group is literally exploding with shared photos and old movies and memories.

February 8
Wayne has become concerned about me. He sees me stay in the office until 4 or 4:30 every day, then come downstairs to try to figure out what to fix for supper. I've got to be more efficient and purposeful with my time and meal planning. I'm so tightly scheduled that last week's funeral put me behind. But I gained so much: more family stories, cementing a bond with Donnie, getting to know Larry's girls, loving Wayne even more. It was a win, even while a loss.

Tuesday, February 16
A rare night of uninterrupted sleep. I woke up to words running through my head and, oddly, joy. The gift of flexibility in attitude. I learned the meaning of those words just yesterday as the Midwest coped with record low temperatures and windchills, rolling blackouts and waves of snow showers.

I learned the gift of being flexible to change as one calendar event after another disappeared from my week. Many of us are back to the bottom square on Maslow's hierarchy, focusing yet again on survival, as if the pandemic hadn't already placed us there for the past year.

The ear worms taunt me still in daylight with the lyrics to last night's virtual chorus rehearsal of "Heart and Soul," side by side with the television drug ad that has engraved the words "magillary thyroid" in my head. The odd, looping refrains give rise to the realization that it's okay to finally love myself for all the "thens" and "nows." I'm back home. I can rest and savor life. I can accept the DNA that seems to dictate my workaholism, my family's heart problems and relationship dramas. I'm ready for God to do His thing. I surrender. I'm finally ready for the final act, the ultimate redemption.

February 17

Ash Wednesday. Yesterday when I was meeting on Zoom with Roger, a new client and his wife, I found myself being truly joyful and realized I love coaching, teaching, and helping people realize their dreams. This is part of who I'm meant to be.

February 24

Lord, I desperately need focus right now but how to do that after a lifetime of squirming and switch-tasking? How can I be still and know God when I feel so driven to serve Him, and to hurry up about it, before it's too late?

Actually, I just realized that journaling is perhaps the only way I find purpose and focus. And quiet. Now that's a revelation.

Today's aha! moment: The world may have needed the cleansing of the pandemic, but will we heed its call? Will we be like the Ninevites and become humble and contrite in time to avoid further destruction?

Anne Spry

Riding Rainbows Through the Storms

Rescued at Last

"*The world needs Christian holiness. We can offer solid ground in a world of spiritual and material violence. Holiness is not the privilege of a few, but the obligation of all.*"—St. Theresa of Calcutta

Facebook Posts

March 2, 2021– *While sitting in line for my first Covid vaccine, random thoughts and reactions...while walking up to the door I wonder if we are all lemmings going to be sterilized. (Ha!) I'm amazed at the army of volunteers, the great organization and traffic control, and the friendliness. I'm glad I brought this journal. I feel like a reporter. My shot time was 10:03. As a friend said this morning, it feels like winning the lottery. At the very least it's a "get out of jail free" card.*

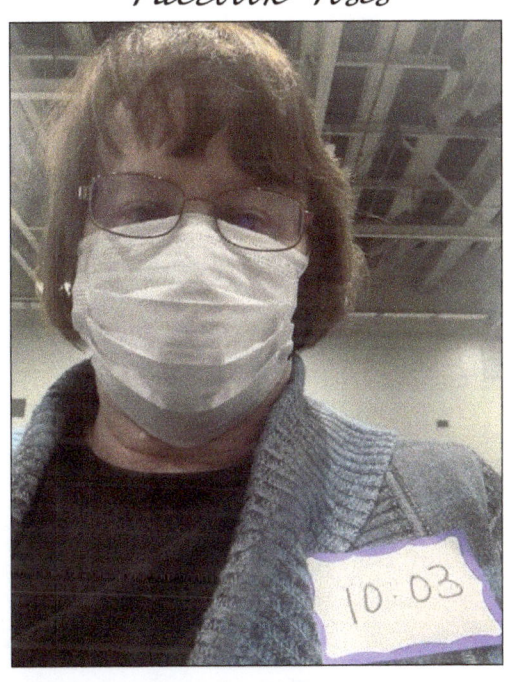

March 25, 2021– *I teased the volunteer who told me to follow the yellow arrows posted on the floor of the Expo Center this afternoon. I was on my way to get my second Covid vaccination. "Why didn't somebody decide to put a yellow brick road on the floor instead of these plain arrows?" I asked. He said, smiling behind his mask, "We tried, but they couldn't figure out what to do about the lions and tigers and bears." Oh my! Okay, so maybe I'm a little giddy.*

Riding Rainbows Through the Storms

Facebook Live

Looking Back at the 1-Year Covid Anniversary Mark

Eleanor Roosevelt said, "You gain strength, courage and confidence by every experience in which you really stop to look fear in the face."

That is what we did in 2020. In fact, we looked many fears in the face during the pandemic as we watched the world crumbling around us. And now, as we watch the world coming out and back into a semblance of normal, we're ready for what comes next. But in true human nature, a few of us (myself included) are already grumbling a little about this new normal.

So what does the new post-pandemic normal look like? What are the things that the front of our 2021 tapestry is starting to reveal, and will we have to live with them for the rest of our lives? What are the permanent changes this has brought to us?

1. Changes in the way we socialize–During the pandemic most of the family reunions, girls nights out, date nights, family babysitting, holiday get-togethers, even friends getting together for a coffee or a lunch date—all of that went away for fears of getting Covid. Will these activities come back? I don't see them roaring back, even with mask mandates ending. I think we're going to be a bit more cautious and selective.

Prior to the pandemic I was babysitting my grandkids once a week. That stopped and has not recommenced yet, due to a number of factors besides living an hour and a half apart. So now, we try to Facetime as much as possible.

I have a new author friend and several months ago we talked about getting together for lunch but have delayed doing so. First, because she had not yet had her vaccinations. That is always a key consideration now.

And of course, with the escalating prices of gasoline, if we have to drive any distance, we have to justify the costs of any trip these days.

2. Changes in the way we shop–Covid merely accelerated a trend to online shopping. But boy did it dramatically affect things in a lot of other ways and I think that is going to be permanent.

a. The pick up and delivery of purchases is here to stay, although there are a lot of Baby Boomers like me who prefer to go to stores in person. One day I went into an Office Max that was nearly deserted and looked around and realized that the few shoppers were senior citizens like me. My son's generation doesn't think a thing about ordering electronics online and having them delivered, but our age group needs a little more hands-on assistance and explanations in that department.

b. Self-checkouts at stores–I think that trend will only accelerate, unfortunately, along with the plexiglass shields between us and the cashiers—at banks, and other stores—along with the Xs on the floor to keep us socially distanced. Hey, maybe that will cut down on thefts as well, who knows?

c. Changes in store hours and the closing of many brick and mortar stores. Our local mall closed for a few months, then began opening at 11 a.m. and closing at 7 p.m. Those are the hours they observe even now.

I'll never forget the first time I finally got out to shop as the pandemic was easing. I had a hair appointment and decided I desperately needed to buy a few new bras. Now, if I went into the dilemma of bra buying for senior women, it would take up an entire Facebook Live and turn into a humor column, but let's just say it is a daunting challenge that requires standing on your head to try to find the right size with just the right padding and none of those danged underwires. By the time I left the store, I was so exhausted, I had to stop and buy a bag of Topsy's popcorn and I wondered how in the heck I ever shopped for hours prior to the pandemic. This stuff is for younger people who get more exercise than just sitting at a computer all day.

And of course, we know that shopping was dramatically affected by supply disruptions during the pandemic – everything from meat to toilet paper. And now that the pandemic is easing, we may not have to worry about the lack of toilet paper, but we get to face sticker shock from the prices.

Another current shopping supply disruption that a lot of us are facing, which I hope is not permanent, is auto parts. I've been waiting a month for two parts for my car. Fortunately, it doesn't affect the drivability of the vehicle. It does however, indicate another pandemic after-effect – a labor shortage.

Spring 2021 Journaling

Friday, March 12

Once again the words of the song "Hosea" resonate in me:

Come back to me with all your heart,
Don't let fear keep us apart.
Long have I waited for your coming home to me
And living sweetly our new life.

This is a time of repentance. And I have so much to repent of. I need to repent of taking on way too many responsibilities. Why do I do that? To please others? To show I can handle things? To use my talents? Because I think God expects it of me? Because I want the spotlight? Do I think it won't get done unless I do it?

Have I forgotten what's most important? Am I stepping on someone's toes or pushing someone out of the way in taking on these tasks? Making up for past errors or omissions?

How can I un-eat the elephant?

Tuesday, March 30

Constipation continues as a personal life theme. I'm suffering from it. I write about it, but I don't publish it. Still, the writing seeps out as I feel compelled to share it with friends. I think it's some of my funniest work, but is that prideful? Nuts? Am I devolving into verbal vomit or diarrhea of the computer? Am I overworking trite metaphors here?

On another front, I am so incredibly pleased with Wayne and myself for progress on the homefront. Yesterday I sought his help with some decorating, asking if we could move one of his eagles that was hidden underneath a table to above the grandfather clock, which he willingly did. Then the three little shelves above the picture windows that I look at every day just got a change. They contained some dark accent pieces that may have had meaning for the former woman of the house. Now they contain the beautiful blown glass paperweights that Wayne's mother collected and that were divided among the three kids. I have brought them all out of the bottom of a corner curio cabinet and put them on display.

Sunday I enjoyed sorting through Easter decorations stored in the basement. I had originally intended to throw some of them away, but am finding so much excitement at the prospects of having Easter dinner here with little kids that I had second thoughts about that.

April 2

I was so tired when we went to church for Maundy Thursday service I almost fell asleep during Mike's sermon. But the music and the fact that 14 people were there made it all worthwhile.

As a postlude, Don got up and sang "In the Garden." I almost wept with emotion and gratitude. The words to that old hymn never go out of style. It made me think of my father and his funeral, although I'm not certain I was in attendance. And it certainly wasn't in Wakarusa. This tiny church wouldn't have held all the mourners.

As I sat through church last night I was flooded with the same sense I'd felt all day. I was in the place I belonged, the church I belonged, the place God wants me to be right now.

Facebook Post

April 4, 2021–So many firsts on this glorious Easter Sunday. First in-person worship service at our church since the Covid shutdown. First Easter egg hunt and children's sermon at church. First family gathering at our house since Covid. The golf cart got reinitiated as the kiddie carnival ride/babysitter and I had to remember how to cook for a crowd. Oh, and the house got really, really clean but no one noticed because we were all visiting outdoors.

All images by the author except the Easter illustration, executed by the author in Happy Color app.

Facebook Post

April 8, 2021–*I got to hold our precious new grandson yesterday for the first time– masked and outdoors – while his big brother and sister splashed in a puddle nearby.*

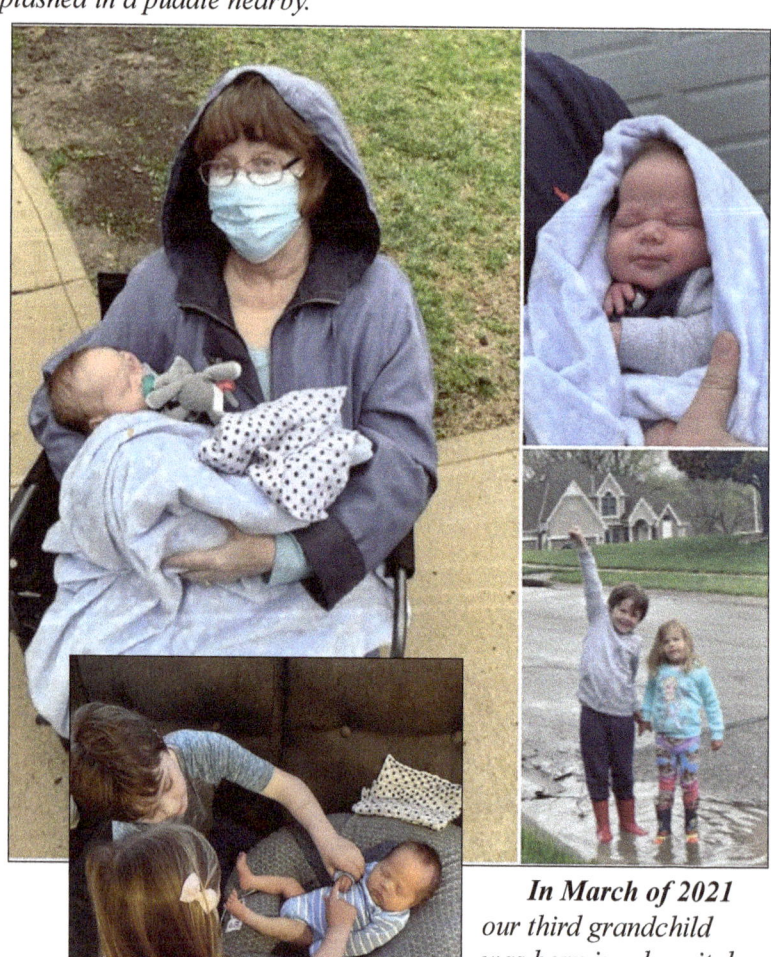

In March of 2021 our third grandchild was born in a hospital with Covid protocols that prohibited visitors, even grandparents.

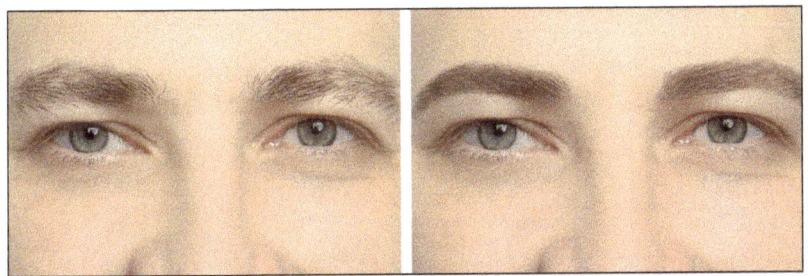

Collage with photos of man before and after eyebrow modeling by New Africa. Adobe Stock #414768374

My first eyebrow wax–From shaggy to tame in one swift pull on a piece of tape. Instant facelift! (Except this is a picture of a guy instead of a 71-year-old female, but you get the idea)

Blog

Living Life Large at 71, Despite the Complications of a Pandemic

"How about an eyebrow wax today?"

"Say wha –?"

With my head immersed in the salon sink, those words offered casually by my stylist were a total shock after a relaxing scalp massage during my bi-monthly color and cut.

She must have been taken aback by the look of pure panic above my paper mask.

"Have you never had an eyebrow wax?"

"Never, ever, ever," said the woman who avoided anything that might involve the slightest hint of pain, discomfort, or surprise. Just ask the optometrist who tries to dilate my eyes, or the ENT who attempts to stick a tube up my nostrils. Forget about a COVID swab to the nether reaches of my brain. It didn't happen. I stayed home during most of 2020 and wore my mask religiously, so as to avoid that nose-to-brain thingy.

"It will make you look younger. Really. It will take years off your face. I promise."

Well, in that case, I was willing to give it a try. After all, at 71, why not live dangerously? I've had to give up my dreams of hang gliding off the cliffs of Oregon and jumping horses like I imagined while watching *National Velvet* as a girl. If getting rid of shaggy eyebrows is the only daring deed I have left in me, let's do this thing.

Eyes shut, I feel something warm touch my brow as my potentially soon-to-be-ex-stylist paints the wax on those intruding hairs that I'd never noticed (thanks to being nearsighted and all). I start babbling about being sure that I'd had my eyes gouged out in a former life and explain that's why I end up nearly slouching out of the optometrist's chair every time he even comes near me with eyedrops.

Soon I notice myself in the same semi-prone position, this time halfway out of the salon chair. Sudden… startling… hot… white… heat.

"Holy crap! You didn't warn me!"

"If I had, you'd have been all tense, and it would have really hurt."

"Okay. You did say it would feel like a band-aid being pulled off. I guess it wasn't all that bad."

Brazilian wax 3D rendering by Argus Adobe Stock #138553769

I settle in for the rest of the ride, ready for whatever she has left to give me on the other side.

There was no such thing as a bikini wax when I lived in Brazil in the 1970s.

Thank God I am way past the age of bikini waxes and only have to contend with having eyebrows messed with.

Speaking of bikinis, last time I dared put one on was 1973, on the beaches of Brazil and I don't think they even did waxes in that country back then. Although they later gifted the world the infamous thong (and I don't mean the ones we were wearing on our feet back then).

And a final, daring dental appliance fitting

For an encore daring deed, I went to the dentist today and had a new piece of hardware installed in my mouth.

The genesis of the five-point dental bridge: eighth grade at Grandview Junior High School. I had an abscessed molar. I could see the pus pocket on the exterior of my gum. I'll bet my breath by that time could have knocked out anyone I happened to have a conversation with. I must have finally managed to talk to my mother because I landed in a dentist's chair for the first time ever. He extracted the painful piece of flesh-covered enamel and I was certainly glad to see it buried in bloody gauze in a metal wastebasket.

Eventually that gaping hole got filled by a crown. And that only after getting married and being able to afford advanced dentistry. But pregnancy, a busy career and junk food does things to tooth enamel. The crown came off while eating taffy and a cavity caused the tooth next to it to become abscessed. Extraction number two. Hole widens. In comes spider partial number one to the rescue…a

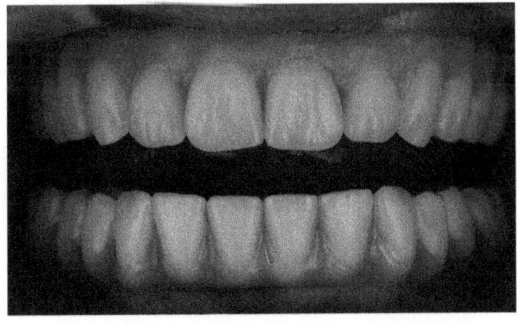

Only an archaeologist will know. If I don't open wide, you'll never be able to see my new 5-point bridge.

cute little plastic thing that clips into my mouth and fools me into thinking I don't really have a hole there. After eight years, it wears down and out. Spider partial number two gets manufactured by the lab. At age 70, I realize spider partial just isn't chewing up my Longhorn Flo's filets like it should. When my ship comes in in the form of the sale of some real estate, it's time to put the final hardware in my skull.

As the dental anesthesia wears off this afternoon, imagine my relief in knowing that when archaeologists dig up my body (assuming I don't opt for cremation) they will marvel at the dentistry of the 21st century.

I'm just so glad that I decided to live life on the edge after coming out of the pandemic of 2020. I got my first eyebrow wax and I have this wonderful new five-point bridge (five teeth in all). I can now easily chew a nice steak. I still need to figure out why my 71-year-old digestive system can no longer handle beef. Is there a wax for that...you know...something to make it slide right on down and out?

New Self-checkouts and Another Death

April 22

Notes on Acts 8:26. "The task of evangelizing a neighborhood, town or nation can seem overwhelming if we focus on our own abilities and limitations of time. But the Holy Spirit has everything planned. All we need to do is listen to the spirit and be ready and willing to follow directions."

Went to Walmart and used the new self-checkout for the first time. Actually had a good time pushing the shopping cart through the aisles, especially when they played "My Girl" on the PA system. I sang along and other shoppers may have wondered who that crazy old lady was singing to herself under her mask.

Sunday, April 25

I woke up with the music and words to "Gentle Savior" on my mind. This after waking up from a nap yesterday thinking I needed to go sing to Aunt Gene. I looked at some of the notes I took in meetings with her where she laid out the songs she wanted at her funeral. She mentioned "Lilies of the Valley" by Alan Jackson but I could not find that on YouTube. Wayne thinks he has it in the garage in a case they once had in the car. We need to find those CDs.

If the weather is finally breaking, there are so many things I need to be doing outdoors. But I'm grateful for the indoor time I've had, grateful for not having to be on the road between here and Kansas City once a week, yet so sad to be missing out on a relationship with my family and with Rosie.

Monday, April 26

Aunt Gene died last night. I almost didn't go over to say good-bye. But when cousin Susie came over to pick up the knee scooter my friend Becca had dropped off for her ankle surgery, she said Aunt Gene was unresponsive.

Earlier that day we had talked to Rev. Kuner and told him the end was near and made arrangements to go see her together next Tuesday. He was going to poll the session members about opening up the church, perhaps for a visitation at least.

When I got to the house about 6:30 the room held four granddaughters and one great-granddaughter. I had brought an old church hymnal that contained one of the hymns Aunt Gene had spoken of for her funeral, "God Will Take Care of You." I intended to sing one verse of it to her, but with so many people in the room, that was not possible. And when I mentioned that possibility, two of her granddaughters nearly panicked and said Grandma had insisted on playing the radio in the background, always on country music. It was her station. If they turned it off, she got upset.

I leaned over, took her hand in mine, kissed it, patted her forehead and told her good-bye. She was in anguish, moaning and thrashing about. I told her to tell my dad I loved him when she got to the other side. I told her I'd miss her stories. I left wishing I didn't feel like there were things I should have said or done or asked.

May 1, 2021

I had a long, heartfelt talk with God yesterday. I told him that I'd spent my whole life in a quest to understand people and their motives, especially myself. I've tried so hard to improve myself and be more like Jesus, to make allowances for others, forgive them, stop judging them. I've tried to become the poet of life I aimed for since high school. But then came the death of Aunt Gene. I asked God if I had failed to take the opportunities I had to pray with and for her, to read scriptures, to sing, to talk to her of Him. Was I too self-seeking? I asked God why violence, abuse, trauma and dysfunction has to be perpetuated through the generations and why some of us are so sensitive to it? Why are every one of us tested?

Then I answered my own question: So that we may find Christ within and know the joy. So that we can share that joy. Some never find it. They seek it outside themselves and get their rewards on earth in material ways and assume that everyone else does too.

Then this morning as I was reading scriptures, I realized I've been asking the wrong questions all my life, trying to understand man. I should have been trying to understand God.

May 2, 2021

I just realized I need to shift some money around and pay bills. And get back into my normal routines. This has been a gut-wrenching, soul-searching, rude awakening week. We've eaten out twice, done more socializing and hugging than in a whole year, and witnessed lots of family drama mere hours after a funeral.

Last night I dreamed of a prison camp. We were playing wiffle ball in the exercise yard with bats shaped like boomerangs, so that everything we hit came back at us. There were obstacles we had to hit the balls over –lines of curled up dead people on skewers, except that in the middle, if you pried up the outer layers, you'd find someone still alive, but just barely. The scene switched to the prison kitchen where I was cleaning out the walk-in cooler. There were bags of French fries in the door, straight and crinkle-cut. Wayne decided he wanted the crinkle-cut, which was a switch from what he usually likes. I found eggs in the door and realized they were frozen in the shell and wrinkled. I took them out and they spilled all over the counter and on the floor and I knew it was going to make walking dangerous and really slippery.

If I interpret this dream, I'd say it's about humans being imprisoned on earth in a haze of forgetting we are divine creatures, spiritual beings. When we strike out at others, the words and judgments we inflict on them come back at us like a boomerang. We cast our judgments and hurl our insults and hasty statements over the backs of our ancestors, who may have made the same judgments and had the same attitudes toward others. Yet we should be more evolved and spiritually advanced and loving than those who went before us. I don't have a clue what the frozen, wrinkled eggs or the French fries represent. Maybe we've eaten out way too much lately.

May 5, 2021

Had another dream and a morning inspiration about Aunt Gene that lifted days of confusion and hurt experienced by the family members left out of her will. After the dream, all the pieces suddenly fit. She loved us all but did not know how to translate that into action. It was Aunt Gene's concept of love that was at work here, the concept given to her by her own family. She struggled for everything–to go to school, to stay in school, to eat, to take care of her siblings, to protect her own mother from abuse. She saw love as finite, limited, only so much available. In her mind, love was to be measured out according to need and merit. She saw men as curses and the women in the family as being cursed. Men were sometimes bullies to be used and manipulated and made to provide for us and do our bidding, or discarded when they didn't.

I find comfort in the quote: "God made us in love for love. That is our reason for being, our purpose for living and our goal in dying."

Sunday, May 9

I have read half of Ruth Maus' poetry book, **Valentine**. As a wannabe poet, I'm in awe. Where did she get all these words? This wit and humor? On one hand this poetry intimidates me because I'm coming to it so late in the game, and yet it urges me on. I'm just so humbled by these new writer friends and what I'm learning about them and through them. And to hear Fred Appelhanz play the dulcimer, learn he's a hospice volunteer and always donates the sale of his books back to the Kansas Authors Club...to learn that member Jan Stotts went to China...all these talented people that have so much to teach me.

Yesterday was a day full of elation and exhaustion. Iced my homemade banana cake and took it with me to the city to share with the kids. Got to see my precious grandchildren and learn that the kids are moving to a new house in early August. From there, we went to visit Rosie in the nursing home. She didn't recognize me at first, but by the end of the visit she was begging me to stay and asking me to put out her clothes for tomorrow. While driving to the city I talked to God the entire trip. I sang almost all the way home. I miss these trips. I want to buy an RV.

Reflections on Our Withdrawal from Afghanistan

May 15

After becoming despondent at last night's news over the plight of the trapped people in Afghanistan as U. S. troops withdraw, it helped to read these words: "Nothing is so unsettling as to see the bad guy win... but a Higher Power has always intervened, causing one tyranny and dictatorship after another to crumble...Time and again the Holy Spirit continues renewing the face of the earth and changing hearts, bringing good out of evil."

And now I recall my dream this morning. I saw the faces of my family suddenly materialize in the fabric of a t-shirt someone was wearing. The faces appeared out of a design like a matrix, a series of tiny numbers. I marveled and rejoiced that I recognized our faces in the fabric of the universe and I awoke hearing in my head the song, "How Great Thou Art."

May 16

Had a good Mother's Day weekend, with breakfast at church fixed by the men. More opening up of things from the pandemic closures.

May 20

Thoughts race through my head this morning, words like unity, the spirit of Pentecost, the Tower of Babel and its similarities to the pandemic, the conversation with Cheri yesterday about how every distraction, even reading and educating ourselves with one Zoom program after another, is keeping us from making traction on our primary mission. With all the client projects and volunteer work I'm doing, the newsletters I'm formatting, I feel like I'm running a newspaper again. I also told Cheri I'm writing a book in the back of my head all the time. But I'm taking to heart her advice about getting feedback and checking in through prayer to make sure this is what God wants us to be working on each day.

And this is where I feel like a bit of a failure. I do pray, but I usually fail to listen or wait for an answer. I tell myself that I don't have Cheri's "direct-to-God pipeline." At the same time, I'm grateful for the wonderful and profound spiritual experiences I've had and know I need to stop comparing my gifts to others'. I have my own miracles, epiphanies and serendipities, my own unique angels and angles.

May 29

Woke up depressed after dreaming of doing laundry for Rosie and stepping on the gas while trying to park a truck in a tight spot on the snow and ice in a crowd of people. All the people watching me were thinking, "Just like a crazy old person. They need to take her license away." And there I was, just coming home from helping another crazy old person.

It's 48 degrees outside with a brisk east wind, cloudy and gloomy to match my mood. I'm depressed about being so isolated from family in general. It's like we're a country or an island nation with border walls and a moat, and no one wants to come in or go out of this pandemic castle.

May 30

I think I may have stumbled onto another theme of my life–the need we all have for control and self-determination when someone else is behind the screen at the controls. We never arrive–either as countries, communities, or individuals–because we're always reinventing ourselves. We have to, because life keeps happening and we make adjustments and often forget our purpose and our connections. And so we start over again. We hit replay. But we are wiser each time. Until we reach the point where it's time to leave the lessons for the next generation. Until we need to leave the light on so they can see the path home.

Anne Spry

The New Normal

The traumas we inherit or experience firsthand can not only create a legacy of distress, but also forge a legacy of strength and resilience that can be felt for generations to come.—Mark Wolynn, author and psychotherapist

Praying, Dreaming, Journaling in June

June 1

Images from dreams: 1. Trying to learn how to play the French horn. 2. Watching a tree trunk of a man, handsome, with long, dark hair, who knew his own strength but was not threatening; powerful and regal. Yet he took the time to speak to and notice those less powerful. He wore a Tartan plaid of green, blue and white. (Was this my guardian angel?) 3. I was working with Cheri part time for a doctor. My office was across the street from the doctor's office and when not helping patients I was writing on a typewriter that had been remade with a wide carriage three widths larger than usual. The doctors let us know they had some patient complaints about our cold hands. And I had not been washing my hands as often as I should have. Plus, I had forgotten to take off my rings. I offered to stop working for the doctors so they could cut their budget. Besides, I needed to get back to my remodeled typewriter. But I had no idea how to prevent that longer carriage from going through the office wall when I hit the return lever.

June 3

Reflection on scripture: The Old Testament sacrifices of a lamb or money gave way to the New Testament sacrifices of time or ways of thinking.

I'm grateful for the wonderful sunshine after 11 straight days of rain. Finally got flowers planted.

I continue to take photos of beautiful clouds and nature and write free verse about them.

I volunteered at church day camp and got to work on a client's book edits while there. Her book is about getting through the pandemic.

June 12

Mary was a woman of prayer and contemplation. We may never understand our lives, the purpose and meaning of our lives, unless we pray and contemplate like Mary did. Perhaps journaling is a form of prayer and contemplation. And prayer, at least for me, was a way of talking to myself at first, because I couldn't see or sense anyone. Prayer is a difficult and challenging act. We try to focus, reflect and enter into a dialogue with someone we neither see nor hear with our senses. And worst of all, we don't usually feel anything. But I've read that prayer is not about feeling. It is about loving.

June 17

Another dream. This time I'm on a trip and waiting at an airport for boarding. I want to leave for a minute but am not sure how to secure my luggage cart and boarding pass. I notice two friends who are squabbling over who gets first access to the door leading to the plane. I approach the woman I know, surprised at her behavior, and ask if I can put my cart in their disputed territory for just a minute. As I wake up, I realize that my role, at least in the dream, if not in life, is one of peacemaking, negotiating, interpreting feelings, soothing ruffled feathers, explaining deeper things, providing perspective, and boiling things down into simpler terms.

Yesterday, instead of chaining myself to the computer to get two newsletters out, I had to get outside and finish planting flowers, watering and rearranging in the garden before the dangerous heat set in. That took me until 9:30, and I had gotten out of bed at 5:30. I then got one newsletter done but the other one is only half finished. It may be the latest I've ever gotten it out. I just can't seem to work fast enough. Yet I'm amazed at the expertise and talents of the people I'm meeting in the organizations I do the newsletters for. Once again, I believe this is where God wants me to be.

Working through July Storms

July 5–Time to accept the "old folks" and the soldier's PTSD observance of July 4–staying at home and trying to calm dogs afraid of fireworks. I almost gave in to depression but just diverted my attention to something else.

Summer Chemistry
Storm clouds build at twilight.
The setting sphere spotlights
billowing drama and promises
to explode danger into our faces.

Mere mortals gasp at the scene,
run to bottle it and preserve it
like a jar of strawberry jam
to taste again in bitter January.

Feasting on this summer tableau
satiates us, quenching our thirst
with the alchemy of Father Sky
reaching down to Mother Earth.

Sunday, July 11

Look at it rain! Had 2-1/2 inches in the gauge from yesterday and now it's coming down steadily. But at least there are no 70 mph straight line winds today.

Finished Jennifer Robinson's pandemic book edits yesterday, after making a pea salad, cinnamon apples and a brownie pizza to take to the church picnic. Then, instead of taking a nap, I did more journal transcribing for the e-book. In the middle of that, Cheri called on her new phone with more of her ransomware saga. She's hoping her laptop was the only computer affected by the hack.

July 17

It must be time for a brain dump. I'm starting to feel resentful that my volunteer work is taking so much time. I'm on the computer so much that I am not being kind to myself or anyone else. I'm sacrificing quality time with Wayne and time I need to be tending the weeds in my garden, time I need for personal projects and writing. I'm ramping up my eating of sweets, not exercising, and of course, feeling overwhelmed.

Add to all of this my worry about my son and my longing to see the grandkids. I'm going to have to bring the sewing machine downstairs so I can make Charlotte's sun dress and do some mending projects.

July 31

My horoscope today talked about romance with my partner but advised against a moonlit cruise. Instead, it urged us to clean out the garage together. OMG! What kind of horoscope was that? Wayne already cleaned the garage yesterday after he found three baby mice stuck to a glue trap.

Me and Moses Whining to the Lord

August 2, 2021

Today's reading from Numbers 11 made me chuckle in recognition. Moses was whining to the Lord about the ingratitude of the Israelites. They wanted meat instead of manna. Moses says to God, "Why don't you just kill me and get it over with so I don't have to put up with these ingrates." (Anne's translation). Sorta reminds me of my drama queen persona when I fall into a reactive despair.

August 9

Humor has been my coping mechanism. Writing humor has been a way for me to consolidate lessons I've learned or get a new perspective on difficulties I've experienced and put a more positive spin on things. If I could chuckle about something, then it didn't hurt as much. The sting of a situation was taken away. And sometimes I could even sting or zing the person that was giving me fits, in a passive-aggressive way. But I knew I needed to be careful not to inflict the same kind of pain that I was feeling on someone else.

Quote: Happiness lies in knowing that we possess the good that we seek.—Thomas Aquinas

I am a child of God
And my needs are great
Help me to understand this life
Before it grows too late.

August 10

The storm is passing us by without much more than a few fat raindrops. Yet the forecast for the next few weeks is enough to keep Wayne out of the hay fields for quite a while.

I dreamed of broken relationships, but in the dream of two women I once was close to, we were reconciled. We were laughing around a swimming pool about someone using a jar of mayonnaise for tanning lotion.

August 12

Woke up with a blog written in my head. Hope I can remember it long enough to get it captured. I'm starting to worry about my productivity. I have so much to do every day, but only manage to cross off a few things on the to-do list. Is it because I just don't work as fast? Or because I have way too much on my plate? Or both? Why can't I say no to people? Why do I over-offer and under-deliver? Why do I not make self-care a priority?

My own prayer (I think): *Heavenly Father, I once again renew my faith in Your plan for my life. I trust in You and love You. I want to be more open and obedient–repentant even–to Your plan and action in my life.*

Take my mind, my will, my heart, my agency and place them at Your feet. Do with me today whatever you wish, according to Your plan, even if it means pruning and discipline. Transform me into a light bearer and an evangelist, a true disciple.

August 17

Yesterday I witnessed up close and personal how God can answer prayers. Cheri and I were Zooming, and she seemed upset about something, but didn't tell me what. She asked me to pray and I prayed that she and I would be able to open our ears enough to listen for His guidance. After the prayer, she told me that when I said the words "open our ears," she felt, physically, as if a plug had been pulled out of her ear.

Then when I asked her if she would be interested in having the use of my Canon digital camera, she started bawling after learning that it could do videos. She had been in total anguish about having to film a bunch of story snippets for her church history project and had no camera to use.

August 26

I wish I could put time in a bottle, like the old song says. This morning I'm going to need some supernatural strength and help to get things done.

I got through yesterday's convention planning meeting on Zoom then drove to Classic Bean Coffee House to meet author client Kathryn

Toure. It was so good to enjoy a truly stimulating conversation and catch up with what she's working on. She has a really impactful, purposeful life. Her husband and her daughter are employed by the U.N. She gave me a book she edited, **Covid Stories From East Africa and Beyond.** *I am so grateful for my clients. Not for the money I earn through them, but for the friendships. I think I need to do this week's Facebook Live on gratitude. And then I need to do a blog to counter the whiny one I did on Monday.*

August 28

I have been so humbled and grateful for the phone calls from friends and family, the kind and colorful expressions and wishes on Facebook and the sacrifice Wayne made to take me out to dinner for my birthday when he really needed to be processing hay.

Two of my Facebook friends called me an amazing woman. That shocked me because I don't see myself that way.

Group of people wearing medical masks #324783108 by melita Adobe Stock #324783108

Blog

Learning to Pivot During Latest Pandemic Storm

Just when we thought we were done with masks...

About three weeks ago I stood at the counter in the kitchen of our church. I was making coffee for the first "Donut Sunday" we'd had in more than a year. We were finally going to be able to gather in our fellowship hall and socialize without staying six feet apart.

That's when our pastor walked in and announced, "Everyone will be wearing masks today and from now on, until we're told differently."

Surprised, I asked why. Let me amend that. I demanded, in a huff, to know why.

193

Apparently, an edict had been issued by the church hierarchy. We were going back into Covid precautions after a few blessed months of being mask-free and not worrying about staying six feet apart. Now we're being told that even vaccinated individuals can get and spread this Delta variant of Covid.

What about our freedom to assemble and worship?

My reaction when our little church of less than 100 members had first been shuttered in the initial months of the Covid-19 pandemic had been one of incredulity. I could not understand how the state government could order our church–or any church–to close its doors and infringe on our constitutional right to assemble and worship. My second reaction was concern for members of other churches who looked at things like partaking in communion and being able to go to a temple as something almost as essential as breathing. What would they do without these necessary and life-affirming rituals?

They gave them up. That's what we all did, telling ourselves it was the better part of valor. We had other things to worry about then. Like protecting ourselves and our loved ones. Keeping them out of harm's way and safe at home. Meanwhile, we tried not to worry about the long-term implications of the loss of freedom. And business owners tried to rationalize having their freedom to earn a living for themselves and their employees taken away by forced closures, all for the greater good.

Like many of you, I stumbled through those first anxiety-ridden pandemic months by getting busy and finding workarounds to this worldwide storm of sickness. But this latest, newest assault on our lives seemed so unfair. Especially since we'd enjoyed a few summer months of eased restrictions, business and church re-openings.

Little did we know that the Delta-variant assault was just getting started.

Learning how to pivot and make different plans

Last Saturday, as I presided over a Zoom meeting of a group of local authors, as we began putting final touches on our plans to host a statewide convention this fall, a voice vote dropped a bombshell in our midst. Based on reports of a significant portion of the young award winners who usually attend our event now being in the bullseye of the Delta Variant, our host district members voted to switch immediately from an in-person convention at a local hotel to a virtual webinar platform. In addition, the county we live in had just declared a new state of emergency due to the skyrocketing cases of infections.

Then the CEO of a local hospital announced that all its beds, in all areas of the facility, were full, mostly of Covid patients, and they were turning away ambulances at the emergency room door.

It's been a rough week in Middle America. And a rough one at our house.

My husband has been fighting a nasty head cold and has been to the doctor twice. The first time he got tested for Covid, but luckily, was negative.

As for me, I'm still coming to terms with the need to pivot and adopt Plans B and C, plans imposed on me and others by situations completely out of our control.

I guess that's the hardest thing to adapt to in the pandemic and in life as a whole. We're helpless in the face of this universal storm. We are anxious, depressed, even grief-stricken.

And for some of us, the thought of once again wearing a mask everywhere we go causes almost immediate hyper-ventilation.

After our author group vote Saturday, I found myself pacing restlessly. I had just devoted a significant chunk of time and energy and lost hours of sleep to coordinating an event that was not going to transpire as I and several dedicated committee members had envisioned it. We had assembled a formidable and impressive cadre of speakers and workshop presenters who were just as anxious to talk to a live audience as we were to host them. They were also hoping for a few book sales and author signings with convention attendees. Now we can't deliver on many of our promises to those speakers and authors except virtually.

Looking for blessings outside 'control freak' zone

I've had the weekend to adjust and assimilate to the change of plans. I'm looking for the hidden blessings. I realize that since this is an event mostly out of my control freak realm, I can get back to all the things I put on hold, now that the convention is no longer at the top of my daily routine.

Now I can actually linger at the breakfast table and have an extended conversation with my husband without rushing off to attend to convention checklists and meetings. I can read one of the books that has stacked up on the end table these last few months. I might even get to some of the sewing and creative things on the to-do list. And if they don't start closing public buildings and tourist attractions, I could even go on a long-delayed road trip.

I looked at my daily planner and started to tally all the meetings and events and plans that had been cancelled or delayed and I slammed it shut. I even put it out of my sight. The thought that crossed my mind immediately was that none of these events would mean a thing to anyone, especially not to me, if I died of Covid. Or if one of my loved ones died. And I sure can't take my planner or my plans with me to the grave, even though I usually regard them as my lifeline to this fractured, pandemic-affected world.

Focus on what is important, I told myself sternly. *Continue to draw closer to God and your family. Prioritize. Get back to enjoying the things you once took for granted.*

The afternoon of the big change of plans, I walked restlessly around the house. All the way around. Outside. Like some crazy old woman out in the hot Midwest sun. I focused on the ground and looked for the Army worms currently causing almost as much panic in Kansas as Covid.

When I walked back into the blessed cool of our comfortable home, I picked up my phone to call my son. Before long the voice call switched to FaceTime and I got to see my five-month-old grandson. I talked to him as if we were face-to-face and laughed with a grandmother's delight when he smiled and drooled at my image on his dad's phone. That baby, and his brother and sister, are what life is all about.

Love. That's what we're here to do.

Illness, child on home quarantine Adobe Stock #329575427 by Gargonia

It's time to look at the world with the fresh eyes of a child. Right now we're getting a taste of what it's like to have no control over the events we might plan so carefully. It's a new Covid World.

Prayer of St. Anselm, 1033-1109 AD

O merciful God, fill our hearts, we pray, with the graces of your Holy Spirit, with love, joy, peace, patience, gentleness, goodness, faithfulness, humility and self-control. Teach us to love those who hate us, to pray for those who despitefully use us; that we may be the children of your love, our Father, who makes the sun to rise on the evil and the good and sends rain on the just and the unjust. In adversity grant us grace to be patient; in prosperity keep us humble; may we guard the door of our lips; may we lightly esteem the pleasures of this world, and thirst after heavenly things; through Jesus Christ our Lord.

Pandemic Grandparents: Learning to Accept a New Relationship Paradigm

School starts this week in many parts of the Midwest. The realization that another summer is almost over causes a shiver of anxiety to run down my spine. The anxiety is for the children and their teachers, specifically my own grandchildren. Most schools are requiring masks again. The Delta variant of Covid-19 is causing hospitals all over the country to fill to capacity. Alarmingly, pediatric cases are rising too.

The advent of the school term prompted me to drag out something I wrote in the spring about how Covid has affected the paradigm of "grandparenting." At the time, regular variant Covid-19 infection rates were decreasing, as many of us had two vaccines in our arms.

I couldn't wait to hold my new grandson and see his siblings, but we were still on the cautious side as we made a drive to visit them. The visit was a bit subdued. Here's what I wrote upon our return.

A masked grandmother and her new grandson
The second deck headline in this morning's inside back page of the daily paper grabbed me more than the primary headline. I could truly identify with the secondary header.

"Grandparents in the pandemic: a lost year, but now some hope"

I'm a grandparent who has just spent the past year heartsick because I missed my two grandkids. And I had just returned from a visit to see them and meet my third grandchild, a little boy who had been born March 3.

It was a warm and wonderful outdoor visit, socially distanced but full of sunshine and hope, smiles, and good conversation with my son and daughter-in-law.

But it was just a tad difficult because we were crossing the chasm created by Covid and navigating uncharted territory. My husband and I get our second vaccines this week. We could not yet hold our new grandson. Couldn't even hug the older two kids or my son or daughter-in-law.

That will all come eventually, we know. But what breaks my heart is that the three-year-old and the six-year-old have grown up too much the past year. So much so that they seem to be carrying the weight of a strange new world on their shoulders.

My grandson is looking forward to starting soccer again next week. He seems especially proud of his role as the oldest kid in the family. When my husband, always the big teaser, asked him how he liked his new baby sister, he expected a heated and immediate retort of "That's not my sister, that's my baby brother!" Instead, he got a silent, confused look. Same response when he was teasingly told, "Hey, your bicycle wheels are going around and around!"

I guess teasing is just not something that kids are used to since Covid came to dwell in the neighborhood. Not since Covid infected the entire household across the street from the grandkids' house. Not since it closed the gymnastics arena my grandson attended and the movie theater he wanted to go to with a neighbor, who was infected that very day at the movie.

Things that used to be superficial laughing matters are no longer. Toddlers have become children, have become almost too old overnight. Ours seem to have even outgrown us. Especially since I haven't been babysitting them once a week.

The little girl who used to beg me to read books has outgrown that now as she allows herself to be propelled up the street by her brother in a plastic toy car, through a strange new world full of invisible threats.

Suddenly, the tears of loss I've been shedding for the missed year of grandparenting dry up.

Instead of feeling sorry for myself and the loss of my companionship with them and memories we could have made together this past year, I ask myself what heavy burdens has all of this placed on a three and a six-year-old?

I've lived most of my life. The costs of Covid are going to lie more heavily on the young. They will live out this legacy. It's not about me nearly as much as it is about them.

Now it's up to me to accept the lost year, the lost relationships with grandkids, friends, and family with patience, love, and a listening ear. I know other grandparents who have endured this pandemic of missed visits and relationships with a grandchild who lives across the country. At least I was able to have a few outdoor, masked visits with mine the past pandemic year.

And the children? In two years I hope they don't remember what the world went through in 2020 and again in 2021. Maybe their hope and optimism will have all but erased the memories.

I know these kids are resilient. Certainly, they're more emotionally resilient than I am. Their ability to adjust and adapt, combined with their youth, will see them through until they can play again with their friends and return to their normal routines without masks and with fewer fears of catching a dreaded virus.

We have to hold on for just a bit longer

That's what we were all thinking in the spring. And now my hope–and the hope of parents and grandparents everywhere–is that all their caution and mask-wearing and forfeiting normal activities is able to hold on for just a bit longer. At least until a vaccine for children is available. And until more of the unvaccinated adults change their status.

On that wonderful day, we will all no doubt rejoice.

.

A New Vista

"A feather is not responsible for making the wind blow…A feather is only responsible for being a feather and doing what feathers do. And so are we, only responsible for being who we are and doing what we know how to do."—**The Gifts of Writing** *by* Hope Koppelman

Learning to be a Fool for God

September 2, 2021

I woke up late this morning (7 a.m.) after many technicolor dreams. In one segment I was cinching my skirt tighter around my waist after discarding a duplicate drawstring that was no longer necessary. I was preparing to go out and teach. I was going on a mission.

In another segment I noticed a tree full of sunflowers. It was in the shadows and appeared in what I would term as a nostalgic, almost Victorian hue, with subdued colors. Someone was selling an arrangement of the flowers from the tree, but I wanted to gather my own bouquet. I was about to do so when I woke up.

I was rested and clear-headed and better than I've been for a long time. When Wayne left to go oversee a carpentry project at church, I was prompted to go play the piano. The first song I wanted to play was "It is Well with my Soul." I have a lot of work to do to master the song. It's in a key that has always been difficult for me. I realized that in all my life of playing the piano I've held onto the keys for dear life, hesitant, afraid of making a mistake and looking like a fool in everyone's eyes. The same with the sustain pedal. I've kept my foot on that thing without breaks, blurring the notes and never allowing for phrases to accentuate the music or the lyricism.

If I'm ever going to play the piano well and master the song of life, I need to rest my hands, my fingers, and my right foot that controls the gas pedal. I have to relinquish control and trust that God will play the music. He's got this. If I look like a fool, I'll be a fool for Him.

September 20, 2021

Hoodie weather this morning, first day of fall.
Breath rises from me like mist comes from the pond.
Butterflies and birds light up radar in their mass exodus.
A feeder full of hummingbird nectar hangs silent.

Pivoting—*being able to move in any direction with one foot, while keeping the other in contact with the floor. Examples of pivots* *recently: pivoting from an in-person author convention to a virtual one. Postponing plans for dinner tonight when our son-in-law had to be quarantined when he was exposed to Covid. Wayne had to pivot in his plans and process hay in a new field when the original processor got stung multiple times by bumblebees.*

October 11

God's timing on everything is pretty amazing and mostly wonderful. The Kansas Authors Club Convention ended yesterday at 12:30 p.m. Now, finally, I can relax a bit, rejuvenate, restore myself, re-prioritize and re-energize.

Yesterday I zoned out, nodded off, did a few scenes in my coloring app, and half watched television.

The long-awaited and much-needed rains began falling last night and have continued today, washing away dust and pollen. It's 55 this morning with gusty winds, a marked contrast to the 92 degree record set a few days ago.

I know I need to do a brain dump, an email dump and prepare an after-action report with the help of the convention committee. But more importantly, I need to say a prayer of thanksgiving for the incredible experiences I had during the convention. I so appreciated the chance I had to connect with local leaders, and loved being the moderator for three panels. I was brought to tears by a few of the speakers.

I know that God and my mother have brought me to this group. I recall the day I went to the Topeka/Shawnee County Library to attend my first meeting. As I walked down the hallway of that beautiful building, I sensed Mother's presence. I was about to give the members a copy of her book as an introduction. I said to her in my head, "Okay, Mother. Let's do this. I know you would be involved in this organization if you were here."

October 13

At 3:30 we're to be at Lake Shawnee to take another look at a used RV that I found for sale on Facebook Marketplace. It is priced lower than normal because of a pending divorce. Yesterday we went to Ottowa to the RV dealer there to look at a Class C motorhome they had on consignment. *I test drove the RV and will need a bit of practice watching my side mirror while turning. It would be easy to forget there is a long box behind me.*

We stopped in Lawrence and had our anniversary dinner and continued our discussion about the two RVs. The one in Ottawa is a year newer and has half the mileage, but it is is more expensive and the interior is pretty ugly and dark. I'm sure our discussion will continue today.

Facebook Live:

Multi-tasking Through a Busy Autumn

Someone once told me that multi-tasking is a cause of dementia. Not sure there's a scientific basis for that, although she swore there was.

If this is true, I'm in trouble. The past two weeks, while getting ready to host two Thanksgiving dinners, sew costumes for a Christmas show and work on client projects, I've done a lot of multi-tasking. I've also been rushing those tasks so I can make more progress on my to-do list. One day, when I was reduced to tears of frustration as the automatic threader on my sewing machine stopped working and when a computer file I was working on for a client suddenly started numering pages with a "PB" instead of numerals, I knew it was time to slow down and do a gut check, a soul check.

My first clue? When I started throwing my sewing scissors and fabric across the table. I was that upset. And I couldn't vent my frustrations at the computer so I spent an hour and a half chatting with tech support. Nothing frustrates me more than mechanical or electronic things that malfunction on a deadline.

Thankfully, that's when my husband steps in and rescues me by repairing something or troubleshooting things while talking me off a ledge. He has a knack for helping me avert a panic attack by telling me to slow down and not push through a task. When he was a flight instructor, he did the same thing with his student pilots, assuring them that they were capable of executing the landing. They just needed to slow down and breathe.

When my husband further saved the day by threading my sewing machine needle (his eyes are better than mine) I realized that I did have the skills to do the task, just not the patience.

We Did Buy that RV

Nov. 7, 2021

First day of standard time. Up at my normal 6 a.m. after another night of restless sleep. My brain would not shut off. I was so tired Tuesday from walking and standing on risers for the chorus retreat, but admit we (I) do need to develop stamina. Last night I ordered a stand-up, adjustable desk. I know I'll have to work at getting used to it gradually, but I'm tired of poor posture and weak knees and ankles. I can do this!

Yesterday Wayne finished hinging the bedroom cabinet doors in the RV so they'll open, in spite of the new queen sized mattress. He also repaired two upper cabinet doors. We tried to troubleshoot an electrical problem that is draining the new batteries. Wayne has been reading manuals and service records. I am so glad he is mechanically gifted. I think he is challenged by this vehicle.

November 17

Yesterday was Wayne's shoulder surgery. We left at 6:45 to get to the city. When we got home, he was feeling no pain, so he used the blower to get the fallen leaves all the way to the road–in the flannel pajamas he wore to surgery! MEN!

I didn't have my quiet prayer time this morning. I'm afraid I tend to regard prayer as one more obligation–something to do as a duty. That is absolutely the wrong way to look at it. Instead, it is a privilege. I benefit so much from my morning prayers, from Bible reading, and from writing down three things to be grateful for. It puts me in the right frame of mind and gives me the proper attitude for the day. And it energizes me, literally and figuratively.

I know our Heavenly Father doesn't fault us for disruptions to our special time. It's as if He says, "I'll be here waiting. Go ahead and fulfill your other obligations but remember to always put Me first on your list as much as possible. If you miss a morning, try to pray throughout the day, at least in silent prayers of gratitude for the one who gives you life and blessings and expands them in the same way that you share your talents with others and spread the love. And remember to always seek My kingdom first."

December 5

I feel as if I'm celebrating the beginning of a new chapter. Or at least a milestone.

Yesterday's Christmas show is now history. I spent all week working on costumes and refining the script that fellow chorus member Marcella Segar and I wrote. I put sparkly silver star duct tape on the Father Time costume, sewed the forest green costume for Father Christmas from scratch, sewed blanket binding on the sleeves, added gold glitter duct tape to the neck and front and sewed on belt loops. With Wayne's help we added a decorative touch to the Santa belt with large white Mardi Gras beads. It was such a different experience to write a script and bring the event to life with costumes and props. And it was so great to have a Santa who played his part with so much skill and the TV anchor who was the narrator performing really well with just one script run-through.

And despite being made to sing behind masks due to a requirement of the Cathedral where we performed, I think the audience really enjoyed it.

It just occurred to me that the mother-daughter tea in May will require a script as well. I'm just so surprised at how time consuming this music stuff is. But it's such a big part of my life now that I can't imagine not being involved. It reminds me of a dream I had about harmonizing with the universe.

Christmas Eve morning, 2021

Each day I grow in knowledge of myself. Yesterday we went to the city to take presents to Rosie and Cheri and Craig. I was so out of sorts, I almost had a meltdown. I thought maybe it was due to my grandniece Lauren's suicide and not being able to order a holiday meal delivered to my brother's family in time.

Rosie was in so much pain yesterday. She broke her glasses again so she couldn't see anything. The nursing home is back to feeding residents in their rooms, as they have Covid in the building again.

But I had a wonderful visit with Cheri and we shared a lot about suicide. Both of us have reached a point in our lives when we felt we couldn't go on and started considering how to end it all. Lauren's suicide has triggered a lot of thought and emotion, but, surprisingly some positive things as well in bringing the family together.

December 31, 2021

I was praying just now and had to cut it short and pray that I could recapture my elusive thoughts later. A behavior pattern of my life has been to hang on to everything tightly. I know this need to control every aspect of my life grew out of childhood trauma but it became a major obstacle to finding God and finding happiness. I held on tightly to everything–the piano keys for fear of making mistakes; men for fear of abandonment, myself for fear of being seen as a fool; my emotions for fear of being hurt.

I need to let go of those fears and burn up the negative habits I've developed over a lifetime. I'm now finding that it is only in letting go of my need to control that I will be able to float like a feather on the gentle breezes of life and go where God wants me to go.

Shopping for undergarments at department stores can be an exhausting, challenging feat as you grow older.

Blog:

Goodbye to Sexy: A Short Course in Shopping for Elders

After months of isolation during the initial days of the pandemic, guess what my radar settled on for that first shopping trip in a mall?

Underwear. Elder underwear.

I was so exhausted upon returning from the Big Bra Expedition, I had to take a nap. It's hard work to bend over and rake through the bottom rungs of department store racks to find just the right bra for an aging body.

Years ago–long before turning 65–comfort became the key feature I sought in shopping for everything from automobiles to gynecologists. The car had to be a zero-entry product with an adjustable driver's seat. If the door frame had a threshold that might trip me when getting in or out, the car was nixed. Heated seats became a must-have.

The gynecologist? She had to be recommended by friends who assured me they never felt even a pinch during a pap smear.

Goodbye underwires that pinch and push up

New bras now must meet similar requirements. Underwires are out. Padding is okay, but at my age, the three hook, back fasteners had to make way for a broad back five. (I'm way past the age of worrying about a male having difficulty undoing three fasteners, let alone five.)

I spent the first several months of the pandemic trolling Facebook ads for bras that could smooth out fatback bulges and hold up saggy flesh. I soon got burned by a cute little t-shirt with sewn-in bra that promised to make me look like an 18-year-old. When it arrived from China a few months after languishing in customs, it caused one of the biggest laughs I'd had during the pandemic. And trying to get into it almost resulted in a trip to a chiropractor (I haven't had time to shop for one of those yet). Chinese women are a lot smaller than American, just sayin'.

That Chinese t-shirt experience and the pandemic motivated me to want to

a. lose some weight

b. order some athletic bras and

c. try some of those things that fasten in the front and guarantee to improve your posture on account of having a crisscross thingy in the back.

Option C model soon showed its impracticality with arthritic fingers trying to fasten the front, in the dark, while shoving uncooperative flesh out of harm's way. Option B model failed due to its requirement of being put on head-first, then failing to support even minimum bouncing while merely walking across a room.

I sure hated to part with these red sandals. By now they're probably in a new home on younger, sexier feet.

Saying good-bye to sexy shoes

About the same time that I should have made the shift to new undergarments for elders, shoes became a sore subject, literally. I blame this on my Sweet Adelines chorus and rehearsals that require standing for hours on risers. Admittedly, some of the agony that resulted in leg twitches, pain, and insomnia on nights after a rehearsal had more to do with my poor circulation and with pulling out of water aerobics classes during the pandemic.

The foot pain caused me to head to a real-life shoe store. The kind with men who kneel at your feet, measure them with that cold sliding ruler, then disappear into the back room to return with a tower of boxes holding your next Cinderella slipper. Except the slippers have now morphed into clodhoppers.

"This is what the dealers at the casinos around here wear, and they're on their feet all day," explained the young whippersnapper (did Red Skelton invent that word?) The thick soles on these models promised cushy standing support, but they looked like they'd been whupped with an ugly stick.

I've been wearing the white and black versions of those things for the past two years now. They are a step up in elderly couture from the first old lady shoes I bought at an SAS store years ago. I think the saleslady became quite offended when I asked with dripping sarcasm if she could find an uglier pair in my size.

Now whenever I attempt to wear anything sexy on my feet for more than three hours, my legs cramp and keep me up all night and my poor feet turn beet red in protest. I have since purged my closet of all sexy shoes. I told them goodbye and good luck and sent them on their way to a thrift store and future younger feet.

Covering liver spots and lizard skin

I am now seeking lessons in elder makeup. The trials in that arena I can again blame on my chorus. For ten years I've worn little to nothing extra on my face except liver spots and lipstick. But an upcoming competition on stage, under stage lighting, called for stage makeup. Enter false eyelashes. Enter things like pore putty and a daily moisturizer. And when it came time to apply the eyelashes for the first time, I had to call in a younger reinforcement with steadier hands.

Someone needs to do the world of Baby Boomers a favor and put out a primer on elder fashion and makeup. Maybe that's what this drivel is. All I know is, I cringe at my younger self for making fun of women years ago who seemed to live in big, flowery mumus. How embarrassing, I thought back then. Why would they go out in public dressed like that?

Today, the judgmental woman that was me is eating her words and hoping I don't embarrass the younger generation when and if I go out in public wearing my favorite new uniform—yoga pants. They don't camouflage my saggy old bulges of skin like mumus did for older women decades ago. But they are great for supporting atrophied leg muscles and mildly compressing varicose veins. One of these days I might even wear them while practicing yoga. Chair yoga, that is.

A Fresh Start to 2022

During the frantic pace that characterized coming out of Covid and resuming in-person activities, my writing partner Cheri and I had begun a massive undertaking. Instead of writing a book to guide people to write their personal histories or memoir (our original plans), we put together a masterclass on writing to heal from trauma. We developed a guidebook and a beautifully illustrated journal and I began using it in a pilot project with a small group. As we worked through the curriculum, Cheri and I began revising and correcting the written materials on the fly. It would take us another year or more to complete and officially launch the masterclass.

I also continued to help book clients and contracted with a few repeat customers who had written new books during the pandemic.

My weekly schedule included auditing a poetry class at Washburn University, in addition to my volunteer activities and responsibilities with Kansas Authors and the Sweet Adelines chorus. I continued to livestream our church services each Sunday and sing with the church choir. And I joined an online metaphysical group at the invitation of a new friend. My days were full but frustrating, because I still had much to learn about letting go and not obligating myself so much.

January 1, 2022

Yesterday I made ham salad with the food processor. It worked just fine, once Wayne helped me understand I had to take the blade off before dumping the bowl. I also gave Lily and Rose a bath and they smell so much better, and their coats are so soft. It was fairly warm and sunny so it was the best day for that. Last night we went to Red Lobster for dinner and came home to watch **The Shack** *on Netflix. Wayne had never seen it. It was the perfect way to end 2021 with its focus on forgiveness.*

This morning I started reading my new chronological Bible and was inspired to give an assignment to my new memoir class to research their names and come up with a word to be their 2022 mantra.

January 17

While reading one of my favorite Bible stories out of my chronological Bible, I became awe-struck by the beauty and perfection of the history of God's people. This treasure is a genealogy of mankind, plus a collection of teaching stories. It is a foreshadowing of today's world issues and struggles. It is the world's original journalism and poetry. What a gift!

February 7

A fresh new week that started with a prompting to catch the sunrise. While doing so, it came to me that each of our masterclasses could begin with a meditation–a beautiful photo with a prayer and music in the background.

Last week was eventful in terms of the masterclass. Cheri was here from Monday through Friday and we were super focused on business planning. But we took time to make two different kinds of bread.

*I finished reading Jenny Doan's book, **How to Stitch an American Dream**. Loved every minute of it and got the idea to do the next Memoir Mentors Facebook Live on quilts. Then for some crazy reason I was online and saw a listing for a vintage, hand-sewn quilt for only $25. The seller turned out to be my cousin Dennis's wife, Susan's quilt. So when we took Cheri to DeSoto to meet Craig Friday, we stopped to pick up the quilt in Eudora. We got to tour Dennis's "museum" of railroad memorabilia and Susan's in-home antique shop. I love the quilt I purchased from Susan. Not sure why I'm so taken with it. Maybe it's all tied in with Jenny's book. I love that Jenny uses quilts for healing with foster kids, hurricane victims, etc. And there's the healing that comes from the creative process of quilting and how people turn to those activities in hard times.*

February 26

A gift of a day. We have no obligations, no place we have to go, nothing on the calendar. May we not squander it. May we find joy in it. I have begun taking an online class on Angels and Guides and learning they are "our extended, loving family." They love helping us and don't get grumpy.

March 14

Feeling wobbly this morning from the Gabapentin I took last night. My knee was swollen so I also took an ice pack to bed.

March 19

I dreamed of Rosie a lot. Is she close to dying? Or did I just dream about her after talking to the funeral director yesterday about her pre-need funeral plan? Covid and distance has kept me from visiting her as often as I should.

April 14

I'm getting worn out by pain. Monday I wrenched my right hip coming down the stairs at my son's house while carrying my grandson. I see my primary care doctor today but need to find an orthopedic doctor here too. I realize that whatever we focus on grows, so I've got to stop focusing on this pain, but it startles me, takes my breath away, makes me brain dead and takes away energy and motivation.

At the same time, ironically, my brain takes me leaps ahead of myself in stimulating projects and experiences. I'm still basking in the glow of last weekend's Sweet Adelines regional competition and road trip with Donna Kready, Terry Davis and Nyla Suffron. I'm also loving the intellectual stimulation of Eric McHenry's advanced poetry writing class. Yesterday, Eric asked me to recite the poem I memorized for an assignment. No one else had chosen that poem to recite, and I just love Wendell Berry's writing. Then the class began workshopping a poem I wrote about crayon colors. The comments were affirming.

April 23

The wind does not know how to murmur or whisper here in Kansas. It only knows how to whistle and carry the moans of spirits on its wings.

May 6

I've had to take some kind of painkiller every night.

May 16

Saturday was our chorus Ladies Tea and I feel like a big weight has been lifted off of me, even though this week will be busy too–babysitting in the city tomorrow, the annual chorus meeting, orthopedic doctor visit, open mic for Kansas Authors, newsletters, Kansas Authors meeting Saturday, then D. J. and Morgan's (Wayne's grandson) wedding. Maybe next week I can really breathe and relax.

May 14–Our first Ladies Tea is in the books. The highlight of the day was sharing the gift of song with our guests.

May 25–Who needs a jungle gym when you can hop on Pop?

That's what two of my grandkids showed me when I went to the city for a quick visit. Their dog Chester got in on the act too.

Facebook Live

Sleepless Nights and Wonky Days

- Sleepless nights due to a dog panting in my face afraid of thunder and lightning.

- So much rain that farmers here can't get into their fields
- All the national and international news of tragedy and conflict.

- Minor irritations like *Better Homes and Gardens* letting us know that because of a lack of availability of supplies, the magazine is going totally online.

- So glad I'm no longer a newspaper publisher who has to worry about supply chain issues, getting advertisers in a pandemic, making payroll and paying bills in a small market surrounded by bigger papers.

So what to do with all this wonkiness? For one thing, don't look up the word "wonky" in your dictionary. I'll save you the hassle.

Definition of wonky: crooked, off-center, not functioning correctly.

Looking it up on my desktop dictionary led me down a rabbit hole. After giving several definitions of the word "wonky," I was led to a "disambiguation" page. Let me share part of the rabbit hole…

Word-sense disambiguation (WSD) is an open problem in computational linguistics concerned with identifying which sense of a word is used in a sentence. The solution to this issue impacts other computer-related writing, such as discourse, improving relevance of search engines, anaphora resolution, coherence, and inference.

Getting directed to the disambiguation page made me seek the definition of anaphora. Let me tell you what I found there.

In linguistics, anaphora (/əˈnæfərə/) is the use of an expression whose interpretation depends upon another expression in context (its antecedent or postcedent). In a narrower sense, anaphora is the use of an expression that depends specifically upon an antecedent expression and thus is contrasted with cataphora, which is the use of an expression that depends upon a postcedent expression. The anaphoric (referring) term is called an anaphor.

Do you suppose that English and writing and grammar teachers are using those words in classes today? I think I would drop out and not even try. Just reading these definitions makes my eyes glaze over.

So back to some grounded reality, I want to offer some....

...suggestions to cure all your wonky ills

• Try meditation. Go inside yourself, get calm and focused.

• Go outside and see if you can find a luna moth or a butterfly and photograph it or focus on that.

• Read a book of poetry or a good escape novel.

• Reach out to that friend you haven't called for a long time and make a date for lunch.

Everything According to Plan

June 11

*It's been a week of progress. Terry Stahl's family history book has been revised and is ready to launch. My poetry and photo book, **Finally Noticing,** is formatted and ready for Cheri's finishing touches.*

Our chorus is going to international competition in Louisville in 2023.

I started stocking the RV and getting it ready for a first trip. I just hope we can use it at least once before the end of July when my son wants to use it.

I'm getting ready for physical therapy next week and get a shot in my right hand to ease the pain that wakes me up in the night (in addition to the knee and hip pain).

Everything is going according to plan, but I'm feeling a bit restless. Maybe it's because I know Wayne will soon be in the hay field and I'll be a "hay widow" like he's been a writer widower and a singer widower for so long.

June 17, 12:45 a.m.

Can't sleep. Had my first physical therapy session and in some pain due to all the manipulation of my legs. But I'm mostly in psychic pain after being on Zoom with Cheri for hours. She told me what the Lord told her, line upon line, as next steps for our masterclass. Surprisingly, it was not to hold the classes online. We are to both hold them in person because that's where the spirit will enter in for greater, more effective healing.

What we have created is a masterpiece...what Cheri has created, really. I've just formatted her creation. The books are beautiful, and they should help so many people.

I guess I feel a bit of a letdown, along with some relief. I was worried about how we could be able to perform when the online platform would cost us $99 a month. Yet we've uploaded almost every asset...videos, instructions, etc. What are we to do with that now?

So many of our efforts have been tailored to the online platform. I'm so tired from devoting so much time to this. And when Cheri asked the

Lord what I was to do, she was told I needed to come to Him directly. She is supposed to start working on Masterclass II, on prayer and drawing closer to God, (which is what I need in order to get my own revelation.)

Cheri and I worked a lot on the Personal Chapters website and I have a lot of work to do in simplifying and revamping that. She wants to see my Memoir Mentors videos and posts become a blog there. But for client work, I need a separate site. But I don't need to really expand my client base as I have enough repeat business. And I have my own books to write and publish.

July 1

What a weekend! Cheri got Covid after taking care of Craig, who got it at work. This is such a virulent, even more contagious mutation. Our first inkling of how bad it has become was during the Capital City Chorus performance when several guests became infected from singers. And last Tuesday a guest at our chorus rehearsal became positive the morning after we shared music.

July 17

A sleepless night made it difficult to put on my walking legs today, but I did it. Just like I'm putting on my observing eyes. Now to kick in my thinking brain or leave the subconscious in charge.

Last night we had green beans out of the garden. Today I will be shredding zucchini from the bathtub garden. I am amazed that the squash bugs have not found it this year, but it may be a variety they don't like. I could even have enough to make relish.

I have found so much joy in gardening this year. and I find myself talking to the plants, weeding more, watering and tending more. I even listen to music while gardening and I think the plants like that.

The kids had a great time today. The grandkids enjoyed raiding the candy counter. Camden went crazy for the balls, and some of us pulled ticks off ourselves from being outside.

Facebook Live

A Summer Surge in Covid Cases

Yesterday a local television news program warned of a summer Covid surge. Well, that surge is already here, if my friends' cases are any indication.

In the past two weeks several people I know have contracted Covid. Most have been vaccinated and boosted and probably had a milder case than if they hadn't been vaccinated. This week I was exposed through my chorus rehearsal to someone who tested positive the next morning after she and I shared music and sang without masks. I have since done a home Covid test, which was negative, and I'll be doing another test in the morning, just to ease my worries.

And the reason I've decided to do a Facebook Live, which I haven't done for weeks, is that I just wanted to issue a warning to people (like me) who thought we might be out of the woods where Covid is concerned. I wanted to also remind all of you to hug and kiss your family members and tell them you love them. And if you haven't taken care of estate planning, advance directives for health care and power of attorney assignments, do so as soon as possible.

For over two years now Covid has given the world a wakeup call. We can no longer take anything for granted, can we? We can't rely on our grocery store shelves to be stocked with our favorite products. We can't depend on airlines to get us where we need to go on time without rescheduling or cancelling flights. And sadly, we can't be sure that we or our loved ones will be around tomorrow.

Yesterday, my writing partner Cheri's husband Craig became gravely ill with Covid. He was vaccinated and boosted but he has diabetes.

And yesterday I was trying to put the finishing touches on this book about journaling through the pandemic when the entire file went wonky. At first I got frustrated and may have used a not-nice word during a customer service chat. But then I stepped back from my anger and asked, "What is this trying to teach me?"

The answer I got was, "This pandemic is not over, so you may want to write about what is going on presently and update that book while you're starting over completely on a different platform."

We always seem to learn things from our challenges, don't we? And there are multiple lessons in Covid. The one supreme lesson I'd like to leave with you is the necessity of practicing gratitude.

I just read an article today in a health newsletter about the scientifically proven benefits from practicing gratitude. I'm talking about journaling every day about something you're grateful for. I'm talking about meditating and praying about your gratitude. It will lift your spirits and energize you for whatever future lessons life has to throw at you.

Thoroughly Modern Mother Mary

August 22

In a dream I was giving a presentation about Mary. It's one of those times when I felt like I was being given dictation. I think I was calling it "Thoroughly Modern Mary," and I was trying to give young people an image or idea of the Blessed Mother as a role model. I was sorting through images of Mary and researching organizations that revered her to try to bring them together in a coherent way that would appeal to young people. Not sure what to make of the dream, if I'm to take it literally or if it's just a message for me. It bears praying about.

Yesterday after church I didn't even change clothes. Wayne and I streamed shows on Netflix. When we let the dogs out after their supper and ours, Lily didn't want to come in. Most of the time she comes around to the front porch and barks. Not this time. The poor, blind baby somehow made her way to the road and a passerby stopped and picked her up and brought her to the front door. This morning we had to lead her and Rose outside with the leash. I feel so bad for them.

September 6

Yesterday as I left Walmart after buying insulin for Rose, I intended to turn left to go to the grocery store. Instead, I got distracted by a family with a sign that read, "God help us buy Similac and food for our family." The woman was a stunningly beautiful Indian. She smiled and waved. I didn't have any cash. I was so captivated and concerned by the scene at the stoplight, I turned right and then got in the wrong lane and ended up on the turnpike. I had to take it all the way to the Valley Falls exit and come home the back way, without buying groceries.

How many families have become decimated by the pandemic? What should I have done to help that family? Shame on me for not stopping!

September 7

Kim Luke sent me her latest mystery novel and I got started on editing.

In the middle of my prayers yesterday, I began to take "dictation" for the preface of the Covid poetry book.

Poor Wayne was running all day, until shortly after 9 p.m., getting loads of clay dumped at the site of the new barn we're building to house all the equipment he had at Aunt Gene's Quonset hut.

September 10

Yesterday did not go as I had visualized it at all. I asked Wayne to get the RV hooked up and the slides out so I could look for the Keurig coffee maker I had stored inside. We discovered the mice had been busy, so we got busy with the vacuum and Clorox wipes and went looking for repellent. I had to wash bedding. Then watered flowers, baked refrigerator cookies and burned hamburgers on the grill. In the office I managed to get Chapter 7 of Kim's book done, did some work in the Writing to Heal journal and recorded a Memoir Mentors Facebook Live.

September 29

Woke up to 46 degrees this morning. I feel so blessed to live with a roof over my head and the ability to flip the switch to heat. I'm blessed also to be assured that if I need surgery, my health plan will pay for most of it. I feel double-blessed to have discovered and honed my singing voice and found a new circle of friends through Sweet Adelines.

October 20

I'm meeting myself coming and going today. And yesterday. Had a podiatry appointment at 9:15, then went to Walgreens for a flu shot, but they only do them by appointment now. Got it at Walmart. Last night I went to our author club open mic and today I have a quartet practice at 3:30 and a chorus marketing meeting tomorrow morning. Have an Author Club convention in Lawrence all day Saturday and Sunday until 1 p.m. but hope to bow out a bit early to go to the city for my granddaughter's birthday party.

On a brighter, less hectic note, the participants in the Writing to Heal masterclass are really making progress.

October 25

Again, how did it get to be so late? Where did October go? Last weekend I should have been two or three places–the ham and bean feed at church, the chorus coaching session and the author convention. I chose the convention.

November 8

Since I last journaled, I took a fun, relaxing trip to Bisbee, AZ, spending Halloween in one of the most haunted hotels in the country, met fellow members of a metaphysical group I have belonged to for several months, and brought Covid home. A majority of those who were in Bisbee contracted Covid. I wrote a poem about contracting this novel virus. Here it is:

Postscript Positivity

Thunder rumbles, rain pelts windows dim-lit
by a November cold front pushing through.
A great day to read a book, eat tomato soup
with grilled cheese, nap sitting up.
It's as good a day as any to be housebound by Covid,
the monster I have feared for two years.
It's a good day to lose taste and smell, with a new
bitterness coating the tongue, while shoulder aches,
coughing and dripping nose bring unaccustomed misery.
While I endure a virus that has changed the world,
will I be different on the other side?
Am I paying the price of self-indulgence
for leaving the safety of rural Kansas to enjoy
unmasked hugs and smiles with formerly virtual friends,
to bond over stories, conference sessions, and local cuisine?
Only to go home and text sneeze and cough emojis?
If I had stayed well, would my focus
have remained diluted, or reverted to
the old arrogance, the old nonchalance?
I admit I knew the world was changed, fragile,
yet heretofore ignored it. Now that I have
met the enemy, found him less than fierce,

will I grow into a new optimism?
The fall shower brings relief to a parched land;
so too this viral bogeyman, now that it's found me.
I have survived–am surviving–this November storm,
and hope the world will be washed clean in due time.

November 15

There's a beautiful coating of snow this morning–enough to be pretty but not a nuisance. My dream last night showed me struggling with overwhelm and a sense of disappointment in myself.

November 24

A cloudy Thanksgiving day and my brother Jim's birthday. My mood may be cloudy too, now that Wayne has Covid. What he thought was a sinus infection was Covid and instead of coming home with a Z-pack, he brought home a special veteran's Covid kit. Fortunately, he has fairly mild symptoms. Unfortunately, that means the grandkids won't be coming over Sunday.

November 26

What a great feeling to finally get my Covid poetry book uploaded. That's about all I did yesterday, besides running to the store. My hand has been hurting a lot lately, making it a bit difficult to do common chores–even writing, and some cooking. I know I need to back off of the fat and sugar to ease the pain in my joints, especially before hand surgery in January.

December 12

It's raining this morning. Another gray day that could be depressing but I'm full of energy and motivation after completing several major projects–Kim's mystery book, Fred's poetry manuscript, the chorus Christmas show and publishing my own poetry book. I also got a really good night's sleep last night.

As if the pandemic hadn't already changed the world's lifestyle forever, I'm seriously questioning the wisdom of large gatherings indoors, especially since our chorus quartet members all got Influenza A. I think small gatherings are so much wiser.

December 16

I'm wondering about my holiday mojo this year. I'm not frantic or feeling pressured. I have decorated gradually, a few items at a time. I have no idea whether anyone is coming for dinner, but I'm not going to worry about it or feel cheated. I'm just going with the flow. Not sure what's responsible for that. The pandemic, maybe?

Facebook Post

Goodbye to warm sunsets.
Tomorrow will demand hoodies,
pots of chili and soup. Some, like me,
find melancholy in the forecast
even as I long for new season flavors.

Riding Rainbows Through the Storms

Epilogue

"In the depths of winter, I finally learned that within me there lay an invincible summer."—*Albert Camus*

Happy New Year to Us

January 1, 2023

When I played a Facebook game yesterday it said my word of the year for 2023 would be "Growth." This morning I retrieved my new journal that matches the lap desk I'm writing on. I'm ready to start envisioning a year of positive growth, especially with regard to spirituality.

January 5

I needed to read the following today:

"I will utter hidden things from of old...things we have heard and known, things our ancestors told us. We will not hide them from their descendants; we will tell the next generation the praiseworthy deeds of the Lord, his power, and the wonders he has done."–Psalm 78:2-4

Enhearten: *a transitive verb, meaning to give or restore strength and courage to. I had never heard this word and Wayne used it this morning I accused him of making it up. Boy was I wrong!*

January 13

I am obsessing about this hand surgery and how it's going to alter and restrict my routines, my productivity, my entire life. I can't journal or make a to-do list by hand. I won't be able to write or format books or a newsletter. I won't be able to feed the dogs or give shots. These are the things that go through my head when I can't sleep in the wee hours of the night.

I need to be praying and meditating, asking for God's help in viewing this as a positive. Just like the pandemic, it will be a chance to rest, go quiet, learn to adapt to new ways of being and doing. And it's temporary. It will be a time to rely on others, relinquish the need to control everything.

January 14

Woke up hearing the music we're singing in the church choir Sunday and the lyrics, "Sweet, holy spirit." Such a beautiful medley! I just wish

I could listen to it in some other way besides having an ear worm.

Had a special visit with Cheri yesterday. Rosie, not so much. Rosie seemed close to death. She had been moved to A Hall because she tested positive for Covid again. She had just finished therapy and was sleeping in her wheelchair, eyes wide open but not responsive. She seemed to be following someone or something with her eyes and listening intently. It reminded me of our little dog Pepper the day she died, when she saw a spirit through her blind eyes.

I felt that death was near for Rosie. All I can do for her is pray and finish arrangements for her burial. I also need to get my Aunt Delora's cemetery deed transferred for my own burial.

January 17

It feels so good to have a semi-clean house and a semi-organized basement. The garage will have to wait until spring and until I've recuperated from surgery and finished physical therapy.

Thought I'd take the time to journal one more time before I can't use my right hand. It was also a good feeling yesterday to get bookwork for 2021 done.

I think I'm almost looking forward to this surgery as an excuse to stop pushing myself so much.

January 18 to late spring is a journaling blank. By the time I got back to it, other events and concerns than my hand surgery filled my journaling time.

Coping With Knee Pain After Hand Surgery

April 24, 2023

It's over now–the event and time and trip I'd been working and planning for, dreading and anticipating for so long. The week leading up to our Region 5 Sweet Adelines competition was profoundly hectic, and the event itself was humbling. Our time on stage was briefly exhilarating.

I didn't know if I was even going to make the trip–not until after I got a shot of some kind of gel in my knee. That was so painful I bawled crocodile tears all the way out to the car from the doctor's office. Then I had to run and get painkillers and a temporary disabled parking permit. Only then did I know I was going. Still, I had to rely on my walker to get around. It was humbling and humiliating to be the last one to enter the stage to perform, after being hoisted onto the bus while seated in my walker. Part of me protested that I was a fraud, that I should be able to walk on my own steam. Yet when I did, my leg started to buckle, my tendons snapping back like a spring and causing me to inhale in surprised pain.

My body has betrayed me. Or I have betrayed it.

May 6

Here I sit in my little garden. A corner of my own, tucked away, almost hidden from the world. I listen to the pleasant gurgle of the fountain behind me. At my left elbow are the strawberries I planted in the tractor tires Wayne brought in. On the old, rusting freight wagon that Wayne brought home from work years ago and that I latched onto now sit the fresh new flowers and vegetables I just planted. I watch the clouds fluff along in a brilliant sky and enjoy the shade of the lilac while a relaxing soundtrack plays on my phone. I have created an oasis of calm and inspiration. I have a better excuse now for coming to this spot every day to enjoy the outdoors.

Just now I admonished my hand to relax on the pen, partly to ease the pain from surgery and partly to let the words flow from my heart instead of my head.

May 9

Yesterday, as I poured out my heart in prayer (mostly about my poor nutrition and my torn meniscus) I felt an immediate surge of energy. I had almost forgotten how real and noticeable the energy exchange can be. Throughout the day I felt God's presence and encouragement as I made better, healthier choices. I'm not sure why I got out of the habit of such pouring out of my concerns, but I know it's crucial that I do so on a regular basis.

Cheri called and I told her about my torn meniscus and how I'd like verification if the deeper meaning of this ailment is one of being afraid to step into the next chapter of life. She called her friend Kim, who is an expert on the topic, and learned that knees have to do with resistance, stubbornness, and lack of flexibility. That's me. I can no longer pivot without pain.

July 18 -Rosie Dies

Rosie died yesterday and I had to write her obit and start making arrangements for her funeral Mass. She died on her 90th birthday anniversary.

July 25

My mind is conflicted and jumbled after Rosie's funeral. It was sad because so few showed up. Yet I was elated to see Marshall's family–his sister, sister-in-law and two nieces.

I have the remainder of Rosie's things to take to charity, but it breaks my heart to just give away family history like the large, framed photos of her parents and one of her siblings.

July 29

Just noticed the surprise lilies/naked ladies have popped up. Yesterday was such a struggle with the Internet and trying to upload book revisions. I never succeeded and couldn't even stay connected on FaceTime with a client.

I did start the morning meditating. Something prompted me to just breathe and close my eyes and picture my family in light, surrounded by love. I was energized after that, but the Internet still didn't cooperate.

September 14

Start with the sublime. That popped into my head this morning, as well as the hymn, "I Surrender All." I had been reading the book, **Sacred Rest,** by Saundra Dalton Smith. The chapter about freedom suggests we surrender all our issues and anxieties and trust that God will handle things. I'm going to trust that He will handle my total knee replacements in 2024.

September 18

Yesterday, after watching the Chiefs game, I stumbled onto a PBS documentary about the history of the Peace Corps. It immediately made me aware of the need to get my Brazil Peace Corps memoir done.

November 6

I lost the entire first week of November by being away at Louisville, KY for the Sweet Adelines International competition. It was a fun but physically taxing event. Every step was painful, from the airport, through the convention center and downtown for meals. I had to get my cane out several times, but then it hurt my shoulders. I'm really starting to wonder how my hips are going to hold me up after knee surgery.

A Personal Crucible of Pain, Mercy

January 17, 2024

It's not even been a week since my first knee surgery and I'm getting a bit impatient with myself. Everything takes longer and I have so much more to remember.

January 20

Woke up yesterday after hearing the lyrics to a responsorial psalm in my dream: "The Lord has promised good to you, His mercy endures forever."

January 23

I may have passed some crucial threshold, a personal crucible of pain. Yesterday was pure agony in physical therapy. When the therapist said if I'm not at the flexibility levels they want for me, if my quads are not awake enough and firing enough, they may put me under anesthesia and bend things to the degree they need bending, then I'd have daily PT. That is a good motivator for doing my home exercises. Besides, I want to transition to a cane and start driving again before I go under the surgery knife again next month. I've got to get with the program.

January 27

Yesterday was a milestone kind of day. The therapist took my mesh bandage off my new knee. And I got a haircut and color. I see light and hope but admit to not yet being able to wrap my head around having the other knee replaced so soon.

January 30 - My Aunt Dies of Covid

Got an email from Uncle John in Oregon. Aunt Beverly, my mother's sister, died last week. She had a stroke and Covid and couldn't even swallow. Now John has Covid.

I have such fond memories of visiting them in 2017, staying two nights at their beach house, and sharing family stories. Then we drove along the coast and into Northern California. Truly a bucket list trip.

3D illustration of knight fighting dragon Adobe Stock #220019570 by de Art

Blog

Putting a Tail on the Pandemic Dragon

Years before she died, my Aunt Gene would end her letters with the phrase, "I'd better put a tail on this and get it in the mail." I loved that colorful metaphor and am going to steal it for the conclusion to this book on journaling through the pandemic. I'm just going to put a face and a body to the tail metaphor.

I'm calling the pandemic a dragon. And on this pandemic dragon's tail I'm going to pin some takeaways, because there are lessons and blessings in every trial we face on earth.

In spite of the emotional and psychological trauma we all endured during the pandemic that began in March of 2020, the majority of people residing on this planet learned multiple lessons about themselves and others. If I could sum up these lessons in one word, I would use the term *consciousness*. We all grew and stretched our mental muscles as we became more conscious about things like the freedoms we gave up temporarily. We became more aware of all the things we normally take for granted, like our family and our friends. Many of us became more spiritual as we grew in consciousness. We all learned how urgent it can be to love the ones we're with and to hug them frequently.

And because I'm so task and goal oriented, it helps me to list all the things I managed to accomplish during the pandemic, despite having to do workarounds and learn new technology. I'll share some of the tasks I checked off my list and see how many things on my list you can identify with:

Learning to collaborate

• I learned to be a better singer by not being able to rehearse with my singing sisters in the initial months of the pandemic. We had to rely on Zoom rehearsals and singing in our own living rooms with our computer mics muted. That forced us to listen to our own voices and strengthen them. And when our director gave us the assignment to record a karaoke song to share with the group, that made us get better in our individual vocal spaces.

• I learned a lot of tech stuff during the pandemic–things like using Zoom to meet in groups and with individual clients. I learned how to record and edit selfie videos. I learned my book publishing software more thoroughly.

• I finished a three-year family history book project with a client, one that we're both really proud of. Much of it was done by collaborating online in Zoom meetings. I collaborated online with several other clients to publish their books as well.

• I started a Facebook group, Memoir Mentors, and I started one for my church to begin streaming Sunday services.

• I collaborated with my business partner to produce what has been called a "masterpiece" of a journal for healing and started a local pilot group that used the materials we developed, things that are being finessed for a bigger rollout.

• I helped form and participate in a new singing quartet.

• I published a book of prose poetry with photos I took and collaborated with Cheri on the design.

Healing things

• I healed from my own light case of Covid last fall.

• I continue to heal from the sorrow of losing people I knew and loved to the pandemic.

• I healed (actually, God healed) a broken heart from at least one relationship that was fractured during and because of Covid.

• I learned to forgive myself and others for judgmental shortcomings, both perceived and imaginary.

• I drew inspiration and hope from dreams and prayers.

• I read and continue to read many inspirational, spiritual books.

• I healed from my unrealistic and even unfair expectations of others.

• I strengthened my faith and learned to lean on God and on all the hopeful hymn lyrics I read and listened to; songs like, "*It Is Well with My Soul.*"

• I drew closer to my church family and friends and grew in service to both.

• I joined a metaphysical group where I made friends from all over the country. I continue to be enriched by these wonderful, spiritual people and draw strength from them to continue to share my own light with theirs and raise our collective consciousness.

• I strengthened and grew in my relationship with my husband, Wayne, and with my writing partner, Cheri. In both cases, we have all learned to emphasize the positive and let go of the "mole hills" before they grow into mountains. We know our relationships exist to make us grow in love and service. Today we are all so much stronger together.

As this is being edited and revised in 2024, the pandemic has become endemic, with little flareups developing periodically. As I endured three major orthopedic surgeries in the winters of 2023 and 2024, followed by doctor appointments and physical therapy, I've frequently seen other patients wearing masks to protect themselves and others. But by now this has become just a minor, if necessary, inconvenience. We all have learned much deeper things from these trials than superficial challenges.

The biggest lessons I have to pin on the Covid dragon's tail are the following:

• *God brings us exactly what we need when and where we need it. He will see us through all of life's storms until it's time for us to go to our true home. He invites us to ride rainbows of love as we grow in faith and consciousness, always becoming more self-aware and increasingly advanced in our evolutionary journey.*

• *Love conquers all, surpasses all and endures even after death.*

• *Nothing can separate us from the love of God.*

When the world shut down in March of 2020, every single person's life was impacted. In addition to deaths, worldwide alcohol abuse, domestic violence, financial crises, and suicides spiked during the lockdowns and social distancing. Students and educational institutions at all levels took a huge hit and many are still struggling. Likewise for many businesses; many have not survived.

When individuals, families, businesses and institutions became stymied by our lack of control over something as big as a pandemic, some of us turned inward to seek the life lessons we're to learn. Many of us turned to God in prayer, seeking answers and inspiration. We coped with our collective anxiety through humor, through forging new directions and adopting new technologies. We read, studied, prayed, and sometimes paced the floors in worry, yet many of us sought reasons for optimism.

Some of us felt a compulsion to help others heal from this universal trauma, beginning by addressing our own individual ones.

We have poisoned our planet with chemicals, poverty, hatred, wars, and now a virus. Our only hope is to blanket the world with the sunshine of love, hope and positivity as we prepare ourselves and our neighbors, families, and friends to endure continued onslaughts.

It's time more of us recognize our souls will live on in light and love long after the death of our physical bodies. We cannot be terminated by the pestilence of a plague or any other calamity as long as we continue to seek the kingdom of light and love that has been placed in our hearts. We are better than our worst nightmares, and even when we can't express our love for each other in person, we can send our love on the wings of kind thoughts and heartfelt prayers.

There is no reason to worry, and never any season to set aside for fear. We've got this. And God has us.

One More Postscript

December 3, 2024

I found a sweatshirt I ordered the first year of the pandemic. Christmas red, the shirt features a reindeer wearing a Covid mask and the words, "Merry Christmas and Stay Away From Me."

The sweatshirt has already been passed on to a thrift shop. I'm not willing to abide by the intent of that shirt, even as friends and relatives become afflicted with new mutations of the virus.

We are not meant to be separated from each other by fear and invisible virus particles. If circumstances generate new rounds of shutdowns and social isolation, we will figure out ways to be together and encourage each other in love. Our Heavenly Father expects nothing less.

Acknowledgements

I owe such a debt of gratitude to my husband, Wayne, for his patience as I came into his world so late in life, only to emotionally "abandon" him to my creative pursuits during the pandemic. He fixed things I broke, suffered through a few of my meltdowns and became my caregiver during three surgeries. If not for him, this book and previous ones would not have materialized. And without his companionship I might have gone totally bonkers during the initial months of pandemic shutdowns and isolation.

A big thank you to my wonderful Sweet Adelines friends who taught me that singing sisters and the gift of harmony can energize you and pull you out of situational depression.

In addition to singing friends, I owe so much to my wonderful writing friends with Kansas Authors Club. Without a network of encouraging, talented writers it would have been difficult to produce any literary work the last few years.

Thanks to Ruth Maus for her developmental editing of this book, Thea Rademacher for suggestions on the cover, Cheri Battrick for her eagle eye on all things dealing with interior formatting, and to all who agreed to furnish affirmations (blurbs in writer jargon).

Of course, I owe the biggest thank you to God, who supplies us all with gifts and talents and leaves it up to us to use or abuse them. I hope this book constitutes a positive use of writerly skills and that it will not embarrass me too much in front of friends and relatives who would never dream of airing so much of their personal lives in public.

About the Author

Anne Spry is a journalist, published author, blogger, and veteran volunteer who has only lately discovered her life purpose. With ***Riding Rainbows Through the Storms*** she wants to share her discoveries on the value of journaling and praying through all of life's difficulties.

Anne has a bachelor's degree in journalism and a master's in communication arts. While she devoted her career to journalistic writing and editing, she has been a lifelong teacher, beginning that role as a Peace Corps volunteer in Brazil in the early 1970s. Even in her 27 years as a newspaper editor and publisher, she was always teaching someone to use a software program or how to write more succinctly. Anne has taught writing to high school students and facilitated several memoir writing groups, as well as being a workshop speaker and presenter for national newspaper, economic development, *The author with her son and youngest grandson, who was born during the pandemic.*

storytelling and writing organizations. In 2024 and 2025 she served as the state president of Kansas Authors Club and compiles a weekly newsletter for Topeka Acappella Unlimited, a Sweet Adelines group. In addition, she oversees weekly livestreaming for worship services at Wakarusa Presbyterian Church and serves as a church elder and liturgist. As this book was being prepared for printing, she was scheduled to begin training to become an authorized pulpit supply pastor in the Presbyterian Church.

Books Anne has authored include ***Letters from Home: A Memoir and a Newspaper Column; Tripping Down Main Street: The Fun and Funny of Community Journalism;*** and ***Finally Noticing: Poems and Photos Prompted by a Pandemic.*** She has co-authored three books, ***Rebuilding Your Life After the Death of Your Spouse*** (with Craig Battrick), and ***Searching for Summer: A Solved but Unresolved Missing Persons Case*** (with Brandy Shipp Rogge) and ***Journaling with Jesus: Writing to Heal from Trauma*** (with Cheri Battrick). Through her publishing company, personalchapterspublishing.com, Spry has helped several other authors publish memoirs, fiction and children's books.

To contact Anne, email her at *AuthorAnneSpry@gmail.com*. For more information on the Writing to Heal masterclass materials she and writing partner Cheri Battrick have produced, check out *WritingtoHealAcademy.com*